CULTURES OF THE WORLD

Luxembourg

Cavendish
Square
New York

Published in 2018 by Cavendish Square Publishing, LLC
243 5th Avenue, Suite 136, New York, NY 10016
Copyright © 2018 by Cavendish Square Publishing, LLC

Third Edition

Cataloging-in-Publication Data

Names: Sheehan, Patricia, 1954-. | Dhilawala, Sakina, 1964-. | Nevins, Debbie.
Title: Luxembourg / Patricia Sheehan, Sakina Dhilawala, and Debbie Nevins
Description: New York : Cavendish Square, 2018. | Series: Cultures of the world (third edition) | Includes index.
Identifiers: ISBN 9781502627438 (library bound) | ISBN 9781502627384 (ebook)
Subjects: LCSH: Luxembourg--Juvenile literature.
Classification: LCC DH905.S54 2018 | DDC 949.35--dc23

Writers, Patricia Sheehan, Sakina Dhilawala; Debbie Nevins, third edition
Editorial Director, third edition: David McNamara
Editor, third edition: Debbie Nevins
Art Director, third edition: Amy Greenan
Designer, third edition: Jessica Nevins
Production Manager, third edition: TK
Cover Picture Researcher: TK
Picture Researcher, third edition: Jessica Nevins

PICTURE CREDITS

Cover: Mikhail Lavrenov/Alamy Stock Photo
The photographs in this book are used with the permission of: p. 1 Loop Images/UIG via Getty Images; p. 3 Valery Shanin/Shutterstock.com; p. 5 Julia Kuznetsova/Shutterstock.com; p. 6 Aleks49/Shutterstock.com; p. 7 Panther Media GmbH/Alamy Stock Photo; p. 8 Peter Hermes Furian/Shutterstock.com; p. 9 Jktu_21/Shutterstock.com; p. 10 Pigprox/Shutterstock.com; p. 12 CIW/Shutterstock.com; p. 14 CIW/Shutterstock.com; p. 15 Peter Etchells/Shutterstock.com; p. 16 canadastock/Shutterstock.com; p. 17 Valery Shanin/Shutterstock.com; p. 18 Katerina Gerhardt/Shutterstock.com; p. 20 CIW/Shutterstock.com; p. 21 http://www.flickr.com/photos/britishlibrary/11181801643//Wikimedia Commons/File:Ermesinde granting privileges to Echternach.jpg; p. 22 kaprik/Shutterstock.com; p. 24 bofotolux/Shutterstock.com; p. 26 skyfish/Shutterstock.com; p. 27 FPG/Hulton Archive/Getty Images; p. 28 Jorg Hackemann/Shutterstock.com; p. 29 Keystone-France/Gamma-Keystone via Getty Images; p. 30 Christopher Furlong/Getty Images; p. 32 RPBaiao/Shutterstock.com; p. 34 NICOLAS LAMBERT/AFP/Getty Images; p. 35 Sylvain Lefevre/Getty Images; p. 38 Camilla Morandi - Corbis/Corbis via Getty Images; p. 39 Botond Horvath/Shutterstock.com; p. 40 Mark Renders/Getty Images; p. 42 Loop Images/UIG via Getty Images; p. 45 Wolfgang von Brauchitsch/Bloomberg via Getty Images; p. 47 Christian Mueller/Shutterstock.com; p. 48 Donatas Dabravolskas/Shutterstock.com; p. 49 DOMINIQUE FAGET/AFP/Getty Images; p. 51 Alizada Studios/Shutterstock.com; p. 52 Valery Shanin/Shutterstock.com; p. 54 Anna Shirokova/Shutterstock.com; p. 56 Maurice Savage/Alamy Stock Photo; p. 57 Martin Prochazkacz/Shutterstock.com; p. 58 Santi Rodriguez/Shutterstock.com; p. 59 Lev Levin/Shutterstock.com; p. 60 Guido Vermeulen-Perdaen/Shutterstock.com; p. 62 Werner Dieterich/Alamy Stock Photo; p. 64 Raj Singh/Alamy Stock Photo; p. 65 g215/Shutterstock.com; p. 68 vichie81/Shutterstock.com; p. 69 Gray wall studio/Shutterstock.com; p. 70 Anton_Ivanov/Shutterstock.com; p. 71 trabantos/Shutterstock.com; p. 72 JOHN THYS/AFP/Getty Images; p. 75 ricochet64/Shutterstock.com; p. 78 Aleks49/Shutterstock.com; p. 80 Valery Shanin/Shutterstock.com; p. 81 Meister des Evangeliars von Echternach/File:Meister des Evangeliars von Echternach 001.jpg/Wikimedia Commons; p. 83 Raymond Thill/Shutterstock.com; p. 84 Leonid Andronov/Shutterstock.com; p. 85 Moment/Moment Editorial/Getty Images; p. 86 Aleks49/Shutterstock.com; p. 88 Hannelore Foerster/Getty Images; p. 92 CIW/Shutterstock.com; p. 94 Kit Leong/Shutterstock.com; p. 96 Raphael GAILLARDE/Gamma-Rapho via Getty Images; p. 97 CBS via Getty Images; p. 98 gary yim/Shutterstock.com; p. 99 Peter Fuchs/Shutterstock.com; p. 100 Pierre-Joseph Redouté/File:Redoute flowers01.jpg/Wikimedia Commons; p. 101 Art Collection 3/Alamy Stock Photo; p. 102 Joseph Kutter/File:Joseph Kutter Tête de Clown.jpg/Wikimedia Commons; p. 104 Loop Images/UIG via Getty Images; p. 106 Lukas Schulze - UEFA/UEFA via Getty Images; p. 107 Reuter Raymond/Sygma via Getty Images; p. 109 beijersbergen/Shutterstock.com; p. 110 Valery Shanin/Shutterstock.com; p. 111 Sabino Parente/Shutterstock.com; p. 114 Christian Ries/File:Nospelt Luxembourg Eemaischen 03.jpg/Wikimedia Commons/CC BY-SA 3.0; p. 115 Sylvain Lefevre/Getty Images; p. 118 Manfred Vollmer/imageBROKER/Getty Images; p. 119 jsorde/Shutterstock.com; p. 120 AP Photo/U.S. Signal Corps; p. 122 Christian Mueller/Shutterstock.com; p. 124 margouillat photo/Shutterstock.com; p. 125 Maurice ROUGEMONT/Gamma-Rapho via Getty Images; p. 126 timkouroff/Shutterstock.com; p. 127 MinhThuan/Shutterstock.com; p. 129 Westend61 GmbH/Alamy Stock Photo; p. 130 Pawel Strykowski/Shutterstock.com; p. 131 Goskova Tatiana/Shutterstock.com.

PRECEDING PAGE

View towards the medieval Ville Haute from the River Alzette in the Grund district of Luxembourg City.

Printed in the United States of America

CONTENTS

LUXEMBOURG TODAY

THERE'S SOMETHING UNIQUE ABOUT LUXEMBOURG.
It's a very small country, but not the smallest in the world. It's an old country, but not the oldest. It's a very wealthy country, almost but not quite the richest. It's a rather happy country, in general, but not the happiest. So—what's so special about Luxembourg?

This tiny European nation, landlocked between France, Germany, and Belgium, is the only remaining grand duchy in the world. A duchy is a European term for a territory ruled by a duke or duchess. Today, there are no reigning dukes or duchesses left in Europe, and therefore no sovereign (independent nation) duchies either.

A grand duchy is a bit more exalted—it's a place ruled by a grand duke or grand duchess. The difference is a matter of rank in the hierarchy of the European aristocracy, which in times past was a matter of enormous importance (and no doubt still is in certain social circles). A grand duke is the third-highest monarchic rank, after emperor and king, and is considered royalty. A mere duke is nothing to sneeze at, but is of a lower rank, and usually not a royal. Today, dukes and duchesses remain,

The Gëlle Fra (Luxembourgish for "Golden Lady") stands high atop the Monument of Remembrance, a war memorial in Luxembourg City.

particularly in Great Britain, as inherited titles that bestow prestige and privilege, but little else.

Being the sole remaining grand duchy connects Luxembourg to its roots in medieval Europe. This distinction carries a certain Old World sensibility and charm that Luxembourgers are understandably proud of. The country is ruled by His Royal Highness Henri, Grand Duke of Luxembourg, who has reigned since October 7, 2000. Henri, whose full name is Henri Albert Gabriel Félix Marie Guillaume, was born in 1955 at Betzdorf Castle, his family's hereditary home in eastern Luxembourg. Henri has enough royal accreditation to satisfy any medieval monarch—his full title is, or was, His Royal Highness Henri, by the Grace of God, Grand Duke of Luxembourg, Duke of Nassau, Count Palatine of the Rhine, Count of Sayn, Königstein, Katzenelnbogen and Diez, Burgrave of Hammerstein, Lord of Mahlberg, Wiesbaden, Idstein, Merenberg, Limburg and Eppstein. However, upon ascending to the throne, Henri dropped the "by the Grace of God" part and officially goes by the simpler "Henri, Grand Duke of Luxembourg, Duke of Nassau."

For all that, the grand duke is a thoroughly modern person, and the Grand Duchy of Luxembourg is a thoroughly modern country. It's one of the wealthiest, safest, and healthiest of places. That being the case, it stands to reason that it's also one of the happiest.

In the UN 2017 World Happiness Report, Luxembourg was number 18 out of 155 countries. This annual report measures variables—standard of living, social support, life expectancy, freedom to make life choices, generosity, and trust—to determine the general well-being of each country's people. Luxembourg owes its 18th place mainly to its very high standard of living (2nd), high healthy life expectancy (9th), level of trust (11th), and perceived

freedom to make life choices (15th). Naturally, one report can't capture the true essence of a nation and its people, but many other indicators suggest that Luxembourg is doing very well.

But Luxemburg does have its quirks. For one thing, it's a tri-lingual society, with most people speaking all three official languages—French, German, and Luxembourgish. Three languages is quite a lot for such a tiny country, but so far, the arrangement seems to work. Another oddity is the fact that half its workforce commutes in from neighboring countries every day. Thousands of French, Germans, and Belgians cross the border regularly to jobs in the grand duchy. In addition, nearly half of Luxembourg's permanent residents are foreigners.

There are many other fascinating things, and many are revealed in this book. Hop right in—and, by the way, Luxembourg has a festival devoted to just that—hopping!

A couple enjoys the view of Echternach, the oldest town in Luxembourg. This charming village in the "Little Switzerland" region is situated on the River Sauer that forms the border between Luxembourg and Germany.

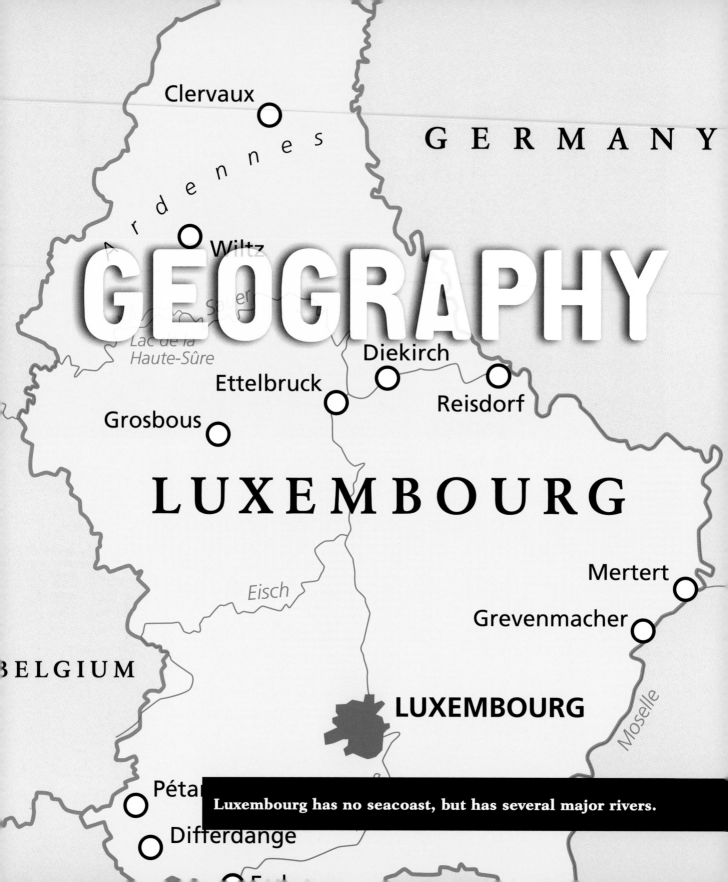

GEOGRAPHY

Clervaux

GERMANY

Ardennes

Wiltz

Sauer

Lac de la
Haute-Sûre

Diekirch

Ettelbruck

Reisdorf

Grosbous

LUXEMBOURG

Eisch

Mertert

Grevenmacher

BELGIUM

Moselle

LUXEMBOURG

Péta

Luxembourg has no seacoast, but has several major rivers.

Differdange

L UXEMBOURG IS ONE OF THE smallest countries in the world. On most lists, it comes in at number 168 out of 195 sovereign nations. With a land area of 998 square miles (2,585 square km), it's smaller than the state of Rhode Island, the smallest of the United States.

Luxembourg lies in a part of Europe called the "Low Countries." This is a very old name for the northwestern coastal region on the North Sea

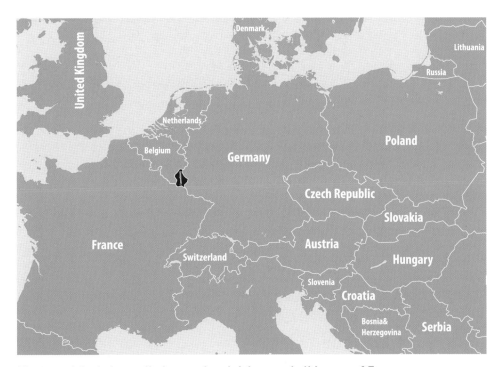

The grand duchy's small size can be plainly seen in this map of Europe.

The fully restored Vianden Castle, which dates to the tenth century, overlooks the village and the River Our in the hilly north of Luxembourg.

where much of the land is at or below sea level. It has no strict boundaries but typically includes the Netherlands, Belgium, and Luxembourg. Today those three nations are collectively known as the Benelux countries, a term that arose from trading partnerships established after World War II.

Luxembourg measures 55 miles (89 km) long and 35 miles (56 km) wide. It borders Belgium in the north and west, Germany in the east, and France in the south—with 221 miles (356 km) of borders, the country is completely landlocked.

Despite its small size, Luxembourg has a varied topography, with two main features in the landscape. The northern section of the country is formed by part of the plateau of the Ardennes, where the mountains range from 1,293 to almost 1,837 feet (394—560 m) high. The rest of the country is made up of undulating countryside with broad valleys. The capital, Luxembourg City, is located in this southern part of the country.

Vianden Castle is one of the largest fortified castles in Western Europe. Built on a rocky promontory overlooking the town of Vianden, about 328 feet (100 m) above the Our River,

the castle exhibits romanesque and gothic architural features. It was the residence of royal families until 1820, when King William I sold it. The new owner began demolishing it, selling off bits and pieces, until the fortress was a ruin (depicted in this 1834 drawing by Nicolas Liez).

During WWII, the castle served as a defense location for the Luxembourg Resistance fighting the Nazis in the 1944 Battle of Vianden. The fortress was finally restored beginning in 1977 and is now a major tourist attraction, open to the public.

THE LUXEMBOURG ARDENNES

The most prominent landmark, the high plateau of the Ardennes in the north, took nature millions of years to carve. At its highest point, it reaches a height of 1,837 feet (560 m). Commonly known as the Oesling, (Ösling) the Ardennes region covers 320 square miles (828 square km), about 32 percent of the entire country.

Rugged scenery predominates in the Ardennes because river erosion over thousands of years has left a varied, low-mountain landscape, densely covered with vegetation, sometimes with considerable variations in height. These differences in relief, together with stretches of water interspersed with forests, fields, and pastures, are the main features that make the landscape so distinctive. Typical of this high area, however, is infertile soil and poor drainage, resulting in numerous peat bogs that were once excavated for fuel. These factors, combined with heavy rainfall and frost, made this an inhospitable environment for the first settlers.

Even today, the living conditions in such an environment are not particularly inviting. Nevertheless, some 7,800 people make their living off the land, either through forestry, small-scale farming, or environmental work. Because the soil is so difficult to cultivate, most of the land is used for cattle pasture. The Ardennes region also includes the Upper Sûre Natural Park, an important conservation area and a hikers' retreat.

THE GOOD LAND

South of the Sûre River, the country is known as the Gutland (Guttland), meaning "Good Land." This region covers slightly over two-thirds of the country. The terrain gently rises and falls with an average elevation of 700 feet (213 m). River erosion in this area has created deep gorges and caves, resulting in some spectacular scenery.

Rolled hay bales lie in a freshly cut wheat field in the Moselle Region of Luxembourg.

Agriculture is the main activity, as the word "Gutland" refers to its fertile soils and the warm, dry summers experienced in this part of the duchy compared with the Oesling region.

As a result, vegetables and such fruits as strawberries, apples, plums, and cherries are grown in large quantities.

In the extreme south of the country lies "the land of the red rocks," a reference to the deposits of minerals found there. Rich in iron ore—sought after and exploited from Roman, if not earlier, times—the area is a mining and heavy-industry region that stretches for over 12.4 miles (20 km). The tall chimneys of the iron and steel works are typical landmarks of the industrial south.

To the east lies the grape-growing valley of the Moselle River. Numerous villages nestle in the deep valleys and behind the vineyards along the riverbanks. Every village has at least one winery. Also in the east, around the town of Echternach, is the "Little Switzerland" area, characterized by wooded glens and ravines with unusual rock formations.

RIVERS AND LAKES

Luxembourg has a number of minor rivers, such as the Eisch, the Alzette, and the Pétrusse, but the main river is the Moselle with its tributaries—the Sûre and the Our. Together, their courses serve as a natural boundary between Luxembourg and Germany. Many of Luxembourg's medieval castles can be found along their banks.

The Moselle River actually rises in eastern France and flows north through Luxembourg for 23 miles (37 km) to join the mighty Rhine River at Koblenz, Germany. The Moselle is 339 miles (545 km) long, and is navigable, because of canalization, for more than 40 miles (64 km). Green slopes covered with grapevines flank the meandering course of the river.

Rising in Belgium, the Sûre River flows for 107 miles (172 km) in an easterly direction through Luxembourg and into the Moselle. Its sinuous course essentially cuts Luxembourg from east to west. The Our River flows along the northeastern border and joins the Sûre after 31 miles (50 km). Its valley is surrounded by unspoiled countryside.

The Upper Sûre Lake is the largest stretch of water in the grand duchy. Ringed with luxuriant vegetation and peaceful creeks, the lake is a center for such water sports as sailing, canoeing, and kayaking. The many outdoor activities, which make it an attractive spot for visitors, have led to the growth of a local crafts industry.

The town of Esch-sur-Sûre sits at one end of the lake. Immediately above it the river has been dammed to form a hydroelectric reservoir extending some 6 miles (10 km) up the valley. The Upper Sûre dam was built in the 1960s to meet the country's drinking water requirements.

The Dillingen Bridge over the Sauer (Sûre) River connects Luxembourg and Germany.

CLIMATE

Luxembourg is part of the West European Continental climatic region and so enjoys a temperate climate without great extremes. Winters are mild, summers fairly cool, and rainfall is high.

The northern and southern regions, however, have somewhat different seasonal weathers. In the north there is considerable influence from the Atlantic systems, in which the passage of frequent pressure depressions gives rise to unstable weather conditions. This results in changeable weather with constant overcast skies and considerable drizzle in the winter.

Luxembourg's rainfall reaches 49 inches (125 cm) a year in some areas. In the summer, excessive heat is rare and temperature levels drop noticeably at night. Luxembourg's low temperatures and humidity make for what those living in the northern part of the country call, optimistically, an "invigorating climate."

In the south, although the rainfall is not significantly lower, at around 32 inches (80 cm), and the winters are no milder, the principal difference is in the higher summer temperatures, especially in the Moselle Valley.

Crops, especially wine grapes, thrive there. With a mean annual temperature of 50°F (10°C), the sunniest months are May to August. In spring, the countryside is a riot of bright wildflowers and fragrant fruit blossoms.

FLORA AND FAUNA

Luxembourg's flora is determined by the country's location at the border between the Atlantic-European and Central European vegetation zones. In the north, beech and oak trees are plentiful. The oak trees can grow to 100—150 feet (30—45 m) high, with diameters of 4—8 feet (1.2—2.4 m). They yield large quantities of excellent hardwood lumber highly prized for its strength, durability, and beauty.

Along the riverbanks, species like black alder and willow can be found. Alder wood is pale yellow to reddish brown, fine-textured, and durable even under water. It is often used in furniture and guitar making. It is also an important timber tree, mainly because of its disease-resistant properties. Willow trees can reach a height of 65 feet (20 m) and are valued for ornamental landscaping purposes and for basket weaving.

A European otter.

The narrow, deeply incised valleys of the north also provide a habitat for rare plants and animals, especially the otter, a protected species. In the industrial south, among the abandoned quarries and deserted open-pit mines, nature has rebounded and flowers bloom everywhere.

MAJOR CITIES

With Luxembourg's small area and population, the only major metropolitan city is the capital itself, Luxembourg City. Nevertheless, there are twelve official cities in the country, many of them with populations low enough to qualify as small towns. Most of these small cities are located in the southeastern region near the French border, which is sometimes called the Land of the Red Rocks, in the area of Esch-Sur-Alzette.

The old town section of Luxembourg City reflects in the Alzette River in the springtime.

LUXEMBOURG CITY The capital occupies a dramatic and picturesque site on a high point above precipitous cliffs that drop to the narrow valleys of the Alzette and Pétrusse Rivers. The 230-foot (70-m) deep gorge cut by the Alzette, spanned by bridges and viaducts, adds to the charm of the city. Although the original fortress over which Luxembourg City is built was demolished in 1867, some of the defensive fortifications remain intact. These provide superb viewpoints across the city, and they offer an opportunity to visit the casemates, which used to hold cannons, hewn into the rock.

Despite progressive urbanization, the capital still retains a certain tranquility. There are numerous shops, bistros, and restaurants offering intriguing specialties from all over the world. The combination of multilingual cultural events, its central location, space for offices and businesses, as well as excellent transportation links, make Luxembourg a capital city of renown in Europe. In 2014, it had a population of 107,247.

ESCH-SUR-ALZETTE This is the second largest urban area in the country and the principal one in the industrial south. The town lies on the French border, about 9.3 miles (15 km) southwest of Luxembourg City. Esch-sur-Alzette is an ancient settlement that can be traced back more than five thousand years. Its name is derived from the Celtic word *esk*, meaning a stream. It has an acknowledged reputation both as a business center and as an architectural town, because of its art deco houses.

The cosmopolitan town, with a large number of foreign residents, also has numerous forms of entertainment and cultural attractions. At Rumelange, about 4 miles (6 km) outside the town, is a museum featuring mining memorabilia of the nineteenth and twentieth centuries. The site of a famous grotto of Our Lady in Kayl, with the purported healing properties of the waters of the spring, is very close to the town. Some 32,600 people live in Esch-sur-Alzette.

DUDELANGE, DIFFERDANGE, AND BELVAUX, with populations of 19,734, 10,248, and 5,113 respectively, are all industrial towns with economies based on the iron and steel industries. They are all in southwest Luxembourg, not far from Esch-sur-Alzette. They each have commercial centers, with pleasant parks and recreational sites.

ECHTERNACH This town lies on the banks of the Sûre, which forms the border with Germany. The town of 4,610 residents is especially well known for the dancing procession that takes place each Whit Tuesday, some weeks after Easter. The old patrician houses, narrow streets, seventh-century Benedictine abbey, and ancient walls have helped Echternach to retain a remarkable medieval atmosphere.

City Hall in
Echternach

INTERNET LINKS

http://www.ardennes-lux.lu/en
The Luxembourg Ardennes region has its own site in English, with many photos of its various towns and places of interest.

https://www.lonelyplanet.com/luxembourg
This travel site has information and photos of top destinations in Luxembourg.

http://www.luxembourg.public.lu/en/le-grand-duche-se-presente/luxembourg-tour-horizon/geographie-et-climat/index.html
Luxembourg's official portal has a section on geography and climate, including regions of special interest.

http://www.worldatlas.com/geography/luxembourggeography.htm
World Atlas has a good map of Luxembourg's geographical features.

HISTORY

The American Cemetery in Luxembourg City is a poignant World War II memorial.

2

LUXEMBOURG WAS ONCE A BIGGER country, including large areas of what are now Belgium, France, and Germany. But over time, the duchy's larger, more powerful neighbors whittled it down to its current, tiny size. Today, those neighbors respect Luxembourg's sovereignty, but there was time when any one of them would have happily swallowed up the entire little country. In fact, during World War II, Germany did just that. Despite centuries of foreign domination, Luxembourg has managed to maintain its own unmistakable culture, language, and identity.

CELTIC AND ROMAN RULE

The Celts, early inhabitants of Luxembourg, were an Iron Age people, able to make more sophisticated weapons than their predecessors, who used only stone and bone for tools. They were a strong race of warriors who drove chariots and confronted one another in single combat. But despite their strength and resistance, they were no competition for the legendary Roman general, Julius Caesar, who arrived in Western Europe in 58 BCE and conquered all the land up to the Rhine River.

By 15 BCE, Luxembourg, along with the other two Low Countries, Belgium and the Netherlands, had become an imperial province of the Roman Empire under Emperor Augustus. Roman rule continued until the middle of the fifth century, when the Germanic Franks overran most of the country. By the eighth century, the Frankish king, Charlemagne, had been declared emperor by the pope.

For the next two hundred years, until the tenth century, the former imperial province was the object of continuous fighting by rival counts, lords, and dukes.

A MEDIEVAL WORLD

Between the tenth and fourteenth centuries, the County (a region ruled by a count) of Luxembourg began to take shape. A tower had been built many years earlier on an important crossroad, forming part of the Roman defense system against Germanic tribes. Known as the *Castellum Lucilinburhuc* (CA-stel-um LUK-in-burr-huk), or "Little Castle," this stronghold became the property of Siegfried, Count of the Ardennes, in 963.

Siegfried's ancient castle sits high on the rocky cliffs of the Bock Promontory in Luxembourg City.

ERMESINDE—THE FOUNDING LADY OF LUXEMBOURG

Ermesinde (1186–1247), born as the only heir when her father, Count Henry IV of Luxembourg, was forty years old. She was betrothed from birth to one of the most powerful princes in the Kingdom of France, the count of Champagne. The count, however, married the queen of Jerusalem instead, and so Ermesinde, at the tender age of twelve, was "passed" to a cousin of hers, Count Theobald. During the life of Theobald, then already in his forties and a grandfather from a first marriage, Ermesinde took little part in political affairs.

On Theobold's death in 1214, she was a young widow of twenty-seven and a desirable match, with four daughters but no male heir. At the beginning of the thirteenth century, succession through the female line was not ensured, and so to protect her inheritance she married a German prince with whom she had a son, Henry V.

Upon the death of her second husband, in 1226, Ermesinde began a personal reign that lasted twenty years—a considerable length of rule in medieval times—until her son came of age. During this period, she established the foundations of the Luxembourgish state, granted a charter to the City of Luxembourg, and proved to be a political woman of great maturity. Under her rule, the citizens of Luxembourg gained much personal freedom, including the right to sell possessions, organize themselves, and create institutions. Ermesinde is remembered as the founder of Luxembourg.

Charles IV, the Holy Roman Emperor from the House of Luxembourg, ruled a vast portion of Central Europe. This statue stands in Prague, Czech Republic.

He immediately began to build a fortified castle on a neighboring rock known as the "Bock," at the junction of two rivers, the Alzette and the Pétrusse. This castle became the foundation of the city of Luxembourg and, over the course of time, strong circular walls were built for its defense.

Luxembourg was able to remain independent until the fourteenth century mainly because of several strong personalities who emerged during this period. One of the most important was Countess Ermesinde (1186–1247), in the thirteenth century, who ruled for over twenty years. During her reign, Ermesinde extended the frontiers of Luxembourg substantially, not by war but through the peaceful means of marriage alliances. In those times, marriages were more powerful than wars in terms of allegiance and family loyalty.

Another powerful figure was the fourteenth-century Count John the Blind (1296–1346). By the age of forty-one, he had completely lost his sight. Nonetheless, he managed to increase Luxembourg's holdings, stimulate the economy, set up a new defense system, and build new fortifications. John personified the medieval knight for whom honor, loyalty, and courage were key values. He remains a national hero to Luxembourgers today.

Under the rule of his son Charles IV (1316–1378), Luxembourg reached its greatest expanse, through treaties and his own and family marriages. In 1354, Charles raised Luxembourg's status within the Holy Roman Empire to that of a duchy. The Duchy of Luxembourg was formed by integrating the old County of Luxembourg, with districts in today's Belgium, France, and Germany to form a single political entity.

FOREIGN DOMINATION

From the fifteenth to the eighteenth centuries, Luxembourg and the other Low Countries fell under a succession of foreign rulers—the French

658 CE . . . . . *Saint Willibrord of Utrecht, Bishop of Utrecht, Apostle of the Frisians, and son of Saint Hilgis born; dies at Echternach, Luxembourg, 739.*

843 . . . . *Treaty of Verdun partitions Charlemagne's empire among the three sons of Louis I.*

1506 . . . . . . *Luxembourg goes to the Habsburg dynasty of Spain when Charles V inherits Burgundian possessions from his father and Spanish possessions from his mother.*

1659 . . . . . . *Following the Treaty of the Pyrenees, Spain yields the southern part of Luxembourg (Thionville and dependencies) to Louis XIV.*

1713–1714. . . *After the Spanish Civil War, the treaties of Utrecht and Rastadt share the Spanish heritage. Charles VI of Habsburg receives Luxembourg, which thus becomes Austrian property.*

1795 . . . . . . *After the French Revolution, French troops besiege the fortress of Luxembourg, which capitulates after six months.*

1815 . . . . . . *After the defeat of Napoleon, territories acquired under his authority are restored. Luxembourg is elevated to the rank of a grand duchy and becomes a sovereign state. William I of Orange-Nassau becomes grand duke of Luxembourg and king of the Netherlands.*

1839 . . . . . . *The Treaty of London divides Luxembourg is divided into two parts, the western part going to Belgium and the eastern part continuing to form the sovereign grand duchy. The country takes on its present-day borders.*

1866 . . . . . . *Dissolution of the Germanic Confederation, to which Luxembourg had belonged since 1815.*

1867 . . . . . . *A dispute between France and Prussia over ownership of Luxembourg, called the "Luxembourg Crisis" almost leads to war. France's Napoleon III wants to purchase Luxembourg from Grand Duke William III, king of the Netherlands. Prussian chancellor Otto von Bismarck opposes this idea. The crisis is resolved peacefully by the Treaty of London, which grants Luxembourg the status of a "perpetually neutral and disarmed" state. Luxembourg gains independence but won't separate from the Netherlands until 1890.*

1890 . . . . . . *After the death of Grand Duke William III, who dies without a male heir, the grand ducal succession passes to Adolphe of Nassau-Weilburg (1817–1905).*

GIBRALTAR OF THE NORTH

Over a period of four hundred years, the fortress of Luxembourg was besieged, devastated, and rebuilt more than twenty times. In 1795 the French general Lazare Carnot described the city as "second only to Gibraltar," a reference to the famous Rock of Gibraltar at the southern tip of Spain, which also was repeatedly attacked but rarely captured. Praise indeed for the impregnability of Luxembourg's fortress.

Under the international Treaty of London, in 1867, which granted independence to Luxembourg, it was agreed that the old fortress, considered a symbol of war and devastation, needed to be destroyed. By then, after nine centuries of military construction, the fortress had, for its defense, three battlements: the first battlement was fortified with bastions, the second included fifteen forts, and the third was composed of an exterior wall containing nine forts. The fortress had, in addition, 47,840 square yards (40,000 square m) of military barracks. The dismantling took sixteen years to complete, although some of it was spared.

Thus it is possible today to walk inside the imposing remains of one of the most powerful fortresses in Europe. Some 7 miles (11 km) of the former 15 miles (24 km) of underground defenses called casemates (basically tunnels cut deep into the rock to give besieged troops shelter and room for workshops and kitchens) still exist. It was impossible to destroy the casemates without also destroying the city, so only the main connections and entrances were closed. Some of the casemates have several floors connected by huge staircases descending more than 120 feet (36.6 m). Used as bomb shelters during World War II, they also doubled as nuclear shelters during the Cold War.

Burgundians, the Austrian Habsburgs, the Spanish, and then the French again. By 1506, with the king of Spain in power, the Netherlands had become disillusioned with both Catholicism and Spanish rule. The Dutch rebelled in 1566 and declared their independence. Luxembourg and Belgium remained Catholic and under Spanish control, with a brief return to Austrian rule, until the invasion by French Revolutionary troops in 1795. Through annexation, much of Luxembourg's territory became part of France.

The modern Luxembourg state has its origins in the Treaty of Vienna in 1815, which attempted to reorganize Europe after the defeat of Napoleon Bonaparte. The duchy was raised to the rank of a grand duchy and became part of the Kingdom of the Netherlands, along with the Netherlands and Belgium. Over the course of the nineteenth century, with France, Belgium, the Netherlands, and Prussia all fighting for possession of the grandy duchy, Luxembourg would finally gain its independence in 1867.

TWO WORLD WARS AND GERMAN OCCUPATION

During World War I, despite its neutrality, Luxembourg was occupied by German troops. After the war ended, Luxembourg severed all previous economic ties with Germany, and the grand duchy joined Belgium in an economic union in 1921. Until the outbreak of World War II (WWII), the grand duchy, under the reign of Grand Duchess Charlotte, made good economic progress.

In 1939, Germany, under the leadership of Adolf Hitler, began invading other European nations, which marked the beginning of WWII. In March of that year, in a speech to the Reichstag (the German Parliament), Hitler promised not to breach Luxembourg's sovereignty. Despite that, in May 1940, German troops did in fact invade Luxembourg and the duchess was forced to flee. She established a government-in-exile in England.

Germany annexed Luxembourg as its own and instituted a program of "Germanization" to turn Luxembourgers into Germans. Only the German language and customs were allowed. Some twelve thousand young

In December 1944, during World War II, with Allied successes escalating on all fronts, it appeared that Germany would be defeated by Christmas. But on December 16, it became clear that the Germans had started a major offensive through the Ardennes forests into Luxembourg, which American troops had already liberated from German occupation on September 10, 1944.

US General George S. Patton had envisioned a German surprise attack and, as a result, had three contingency plans drawn up. He transmitted one of these to his army, and the entire force made a 90-degree turn toward the north, pushing through Luxembourg. They hit the advancing German units in the flanks on the southern shoulder of the "bulge," or salient—a military term used to describe the bulge in the Allies' line that the Germans had caused by their advance. During fierce combat, with many casualties, that took place under adverse winter conditions, Patton's army finally defeated the enemy by the end of January. The Battle of the Bulge exhausted Nazi Germany's last operational reserves, and, by May 1945, they had unconditionally surrendered. It was the largest and bloodiest battle fought by the United States in World War II.

General Patton Memorial in Ettelbruck.

Despite this resounding success, Patton was relieved of his command in October 1945 because of the general's fierce antagonism toward communism. In addition, convinced that his destiny lay in military glory, Patton was known for his arrogance and vanity, which, unfortunately, earned him many enemies. Others, however, saw him as a true Southern gentleman, prizing bravery above all other virtues. Nevertheless, he remains a national hero to Luxembourgers. In December 1945, Patton died as a result of an automobile accident and is buried in the Luxembourg American Cemetery in the village of Hamm, at the head of the fallen soldiers from the Third Army he had commanded.

Luxembourgish men were forced to serve in the German army, of whom nearly three thousand died. Although some Luxembourgers collaborated with the Nazi occupiers, many others joined the Resistance.

At the start of the war, Luxembourg had a small population of about 3,500 Jews, many of them having fled persecution in Germany and Eastern Europe. But once the Germans invaded the duchy, the Jews in Luxembourg found themselves to be no safer. Of the original Jewish population of Luxembourg, only thirty-six are known to have survived the war.

After five years of occupation, Allied forces under US General George S. Patton's command finally liberated Luxembourg in April 1945.

On September 10, 1944, Luxembourgers burn a Nazi poster as US troops pass through a town in pursuit of the retreating Germany army.

Occupied by the Germans during World War II, Luxembourgers organized various covert resistance groups. The members engaged in counterpropaganda efforts, such as publishing underground newspapers and flyers to report anti-German war news and boost morale.

The Resistance's most important contribution was the passing on of vital information to the Allies, which influenced the course of the war and caused considerable damage to the Nazis. Penalties for such activities were severe, but this did not deter the Resistance operatives.

Not far from the border with Poland, at Peenemünde, the Germans had set up a research center for the development of a long-range rocket (shown at right). The well-guarded secret base, though, needed a large workforce to run it, which was supplied by prisoners of war. A number of young Luxembourgers, forced to work on the site, quickly realized what was going on. They conceived an ingenious method of smuggling out information about the rocket project, which helped the Allies in their later bombing of the plant. The network of conspirators was never discovered.

MODERN LUXEMBOURG

Grand Duchess Charlotte reigned for forty-five years, from 1919 to 1964, a period of general prosperity for Luxembourgers, except for the interruptions of World War II. Grand Duke Jean (born 1921) succeeded to the throne in 1964 after his mother abdicated. He reigned until 2000, when his son Henri (b. 1955) became grand duke. Henri is married to Maria Teresa Mestre (born in Havana, Cuba, 1956).

In 1948, after the deprivations of World War II, Luxembourg gave up its neutrality by joining various international organizations. These included the

United Nations (UN), the North Atlantic Treaty Organization (NATO), and the Organization for Economic Cooperation and Development (OECD). Through these organizations, and the Benelux Customs Union with Belgium and the Netherlands, Luxembourg has supported a policy of cooperation on the international front and, in the post-war period, has enjoyed unprecedented peace and economic prosperity.

In 1951 Luxembourg and the two other Benelux countries, plus Germany, France, and Italy, decided to form the six-member European Coal and Steel Community (ECSC). Playing a major role in this plan was Foreign Minister Robert Schuman of France, who was Luxembourg-born and raised.

Based on the understanding that if an individual nation does not alone control its armaments and heavy industries, then it can no longer declare war, the ECSC became the first step toward European integration.

Robert Schuman, center, speaks at a Conference of the European Community of Steel and Coal.

THE EUROPEAN UNION

The second stage of European unification came soon after, in 1958, with the establishment of the European Economic Community (EEC), an institution set up to facilitate free trade of goods and services among the six member countries, of which Luxembourg was one. By 1990, membership had increased to twelve. The Maastricht Treaty, the third stage, led to the creation of the European Union (EU) in 1993. It set the stage for the even more ambitious goal of future political and monetary solidarity.

As of April 2017, there were twenty-eight member nations of the EU, all with market economies and with a combined population of some 510 million people. (In 2016, the United Kingdom voted to leave the EU, which it began doing on March 29, 2017. It expects to complete the process and officially leave the EU on March 29, 2019.) Free movement of goods and capital now

A sign marks the Luxembourg border in the town of Schengen at the tri-state point of Germany, Luxembourg, and France. The 1985 Schengen Agreement treaty created Europe's Schengen Area, a region of twenty-six European Union nations that have mutually abolished passport requirements and other border controls between them.

makes it possible to trade and invest money anywhere in the Union. And free movement of people means that citizens of any EU country can travel, reside, study, and work wherever they wish in the Union.

There are also common agreements on foreign, security, and agricultural policies, as well as on justice and domestic affairs issues. An important landmark of the EU was its achieving the goal of monetary union. The idea of a single currency was first introduced at the Hague Summit in 1969. Because of the unfavorable worldwide economic climate then, it could not be applied. The idea was nevertheless relaunched, and the euro came into being—in theory, at first—in January 1999. Three years later, in January 2002, euro notes and coins were introduced and put into circulation in the participating countries.

By 2015, nineteen member nations of the EU had adopted the euro as their common currency. Those countries, frequently referred to as the Eurozone, include Austria, Belgium, Cyprus, Estonia, Finland, France, Germany, Greece, Ireland, Italy, Latvia, Lithuania, Luxembourg, Malta, Netherlands, Portugal, Slovakia, Slovenia, and Spain.

At European Union meetings, the Council of Ministers has a mandate to reach compromises, without any single government being placed at a disadvantage. Proposals for laws are presented to this council, after being drawn up by the European Commission. Every member has a full veto power. This means that, in some circumstances, Luxembourg, or any other member nation, can veto legislation that all the other member states have supported.

The Commission is led by a president who is chosen by the European Council with the approval of the European Parliament. Jacques Santer, a former prime minister of Luxembourg, served as president of the European Commission from 1995 to 1999. Though a European Parliament plays a steadily increasing role in the drafting of EU laws, it does not yet have the power equivalent to national parliaments. The Court of Justice ensures that EU law is carried out.

Today Luxembourg is a major supporter and force behind European economic and political unification. Both the government and the people take the issue seriously and understand that there can be no future outside a European Union for such a small country as Luxembourg.

INTERNET LINKS

https://www.britannica.com/place/Luxembourg#toc214458
This site gives a good overview of Luxembourg's history, including a video of the German invasion in WWII.

https://europa.eu/european-union/index_en
This is the official website of the European Union.

http://www.history.com/news/8-things-you-may-not-know-about-the-battle-of-the-bulge
History.com presents articles and videos about the Battle of the Bulge, with many links to related subjects.

http://www.worldatlas.com/webimage/countrys/europe/luxembourg/lutimeln.htm
This site offers Luxembourg's history in a timeline format.

GOVERNMENT

A statue of a lion, a symbol of the state, graces the entrance to City Hall in Luxembourg City.

3

LUXEMBOURG IS THE ONLY GRAND duchy remaining in the world. An independent sovereign state since 1839, Luxembourg is a constitutional monarchy headed, since 2000, by Grand Duke Henri (b. 1955). Ultimate power, however, resides with the people through their elected representatives. The prime minister is the head of government and the Council of Ministers. He or she is also the leader of the majority-winning political party following elections. Under Luxembourg's constitution, the grand duke or grand duchess and the cabinet together exercise executive power.

If a need arises to consult the people directly on a particular issue of national importance, a referendum can be called. Results of such a referendum, however, are not binding on the government.

● ● ● ● ● ● ● ● ● ● ● ● ●

In 2013, Xavier Bettel became Luxembourg's first openly gay prime minister and the third such head of government in the world, following Iceland's Prime Minister Jóhanna Sigurðardóttir and Belgium's Prime Minister Elio Di Rupo. After Luxembourg's new same-sex marriage laws went into effect in January 2015, Bettel married his partner Gauthier Destenay in May 2015.

THE ROYAL FAMILY

Grand Duke Henri of Luxembourg stands before his country's flag at a press conference in 2016.

The grand duchy's head of state is the grand duke. Until 2008, the sovereign exercised legislative power in that he had to approve all new laws. Since then, however, a constitutional change rescinded that power and the grand duke's position as chief executive is largely ceremonial. As such, he represents national unity and continuity. Grand Duke Henri succeeded to the throne in October 2000, when his father Jean (b. 1921) abdicated, or stepped down. Henri is the country's ninth monarch since 1815, when Luxembourg was elevated to the status of grand duchy.

Henri is the eldest son of Grand Duke Jean and Princess Joséphine Charlotte of Belgium, and a first cousin of Philippe, the current king of the Belgians. In 1981, Henri married María Teresa Mestre y Batista (b. 1956) of Havana, Cuba, who grew up in New York. The grand duke and grand duchess have five children, Guillaume, Félix, Louis, Alexandra, and Sébastien.

The endurance of the monarchy is seen by Luxembourgers as a testament of stability and continuity. Widely admired and popular, the royal family live quiet and discreet lives with little pomp or headlines. Far from embracing an isolated and grand lifestyle, members of the royal family can be met shopping in the city center, and the members of the youngest generation attend regular primary and secondary schools.

Other reasons for the continued support of the monarchy by an overwhelming majority of the people are nationalistic and economic. For example, though living in exile in London during World War II, the late Grand Duchess Charlotte (grandmother of Grand Duke Henri) spoke to her people regularly on radio and became a living symbol of national identity.

SUCCESSION TO THE THRONE

The crown of the grand duchy is hereditary in the House of Nassau dynasty and passes by lineal descent.

Prior to 2011, succession to the throne of Luxembourg favored the first-born male heir. This traditional form of succession would bypass the female heirs. Only if there is no male born in either of the two branches of the family did the crown pass to the female heir of the reigning dynasty. In 2011, that form of succession was replaced with absolute primogeniture, in which gender doesn't matter in the inheritance.

This newer form of primogeniture did not exist in any modern monarchy before 1980, when Sweden became the first country to adopt it. As absolute succession better matches modern sensibilities regarding the equality of the sexes, other Western countries followed suit—the Netherlands in 1983, Norway in 1990, Belgium in 1991, Denmark in 2009, Luxembourg in 2011, and the United Kingdom in 2015.

In Luxembourg, the children of the grand duke or duchess use the title "Prince or Princess of Luxembourg." The heir apparent (first in line to the throne) is Grand Duke Henri's first-borne child, Prince Guillaume, Hereditary Grand Duke of Luxembourg (b. 1981).

Grand Duchess Maria Teresa (center, holding white flowers) and Grand Duke Henri (center front) stand with their children and other members of the Luxembourg royal family on National Day, June 23, 2016.

At the end of the war, her husband, Prince Felix, and son Jean, who later became the grand duke, entered Luxembourg in uniform with the first American liberators. The involvement of Jean's oldest son, Henri, the current grand duke, in numerous international organizations, and as part of economic missions, also benefits the country's image and results in considerable trade and investment opportunities.

THE CONSTITUTION

Luxembourg's constitution guarantees the rights of citizens and regulates the organization of public authorities. Equality before the law, individual freedom, freedom of opinion and the press, freedom of worship, the right to state education, and the right to work are some of the public rights specified by the constitution.

In the first few decades of its independence, Luxembourg lived through four different constitutions. The current one was adopted in 1868 and has been amended several times—the last in 2008—to make the constitution more democratic. One of the most important amendments was the restriction of the monarch's power in the making of laws.

REPRESENTATION OF THE PEOPLE

For the purpose of the general elections, the country is divided into four electoral districts. Sixty deputies have been elected every five years by universal suffrage since 1919. Voting age is eighteen. Elections of these deputies are based on proportional representation among the various political parties.

According to the Luxembourg constitution, legislative power belongs the sixty-member Chamber of Deputies. Legislation is introduced to the Chamber by the grand duke, who exercises executive power together with the cabinet—including the prime minister and other ministers—and in accordance with the constitution of 1868.

There is also a twenty-one-member advisory body called the Council of State, with members being appointed for life by the grand duke. This Council

Prior to 2008, the grand duke or duchess approved and signed each bill passed by the Luxembourg parliament. The procedure was largely seen as a formality because although the constitution granted the monarch the right to refuse, none had actually done so since 1912. To refuse to sign a bill was seen as defying the will of the democratically-elected government.

In February 2008, the parliament introduced a law to allow for medically-assisted euthanasia, or suicide. Using a Belgian law passed in 2002 as a model, the bill defined the circumstances under which a terminally ill person could be granted the right to die with a doctor's help. (Along with Belgium, the other two countries to have legalized assisted suicide at that time were the Netherlands and Colombia.) The law hit a roadblock when Grand Duke Henri refused to sign the bill, which in turn caused a constitutional crisis in Luxembourg.

Henri, a Roman Catholic, said he could not sign the bill for reasons of conscience, as euthanasia is opposed by the Catholic Church. However, with 70 percent of Luxembourgers—predominantly Catholics themselves—supporting the bill, the grand duke did not want to defy the will of the people. The problem was solved with an amendment to the constitution. It stripped the monarch of the power to veto a bill and essentially turned the monarchy into a ceremonial figurehead. Henri agreed to approve the amendment, giving his last official legislative approval.

The law on euthanasia and assisted suicide went into effect in 2009.

of State is not a democratically-elected institution and decisions made by it can be overturned. The extent of its power is to delay and examine laws, not to prevent them. Nevertheless, members are required to discuss bills, and no final vote can be taken on any bill by the Chamber before the Council's opinion has been heard.

Executive power is exercised by the Council of Ministers, presently eleven ministers and two state secretaries, and is led by the prime minister, who is the head of the political party with the most parliamentary seats. The prime minister selects ministers, taking care to ensure the shaping of a cabinet that has the support of the majority of the Chamber. Ministers are then officially appointed by the grand duke. Each minister is responsible for a particular branch of public administration. They can speak in the Chamber of Deputies, but they are not members of it.

In 2013, Xavier Bettel, the former mayor of Luxembourg City from 2011—2013, became prime minister. The next elections are to be held in June 2018.

PUBLIC ADMINISTRATION

Luxembourg's government acts through ministerial departments and public authorities directly answerable to it. Each member of the government is in charge of one or more ministerial departments, assisted by advisers.

Certain public services, such as tax collection, the post office, and the water authority, are separate from the central offices of the government. They come under the direction of heads of administration, although still supervised by the minister concerned.

For local government, Luxembourg is divided into communes, something like states, each administered by a council elected by the people. Council members are elected for six years. From their membership, an executive body is formed to administer the daily affairs of the commune, such as education, public health, and electricity.

Prime Minister Xavier Bettel arrives at a summit of EU leaders in Rome in 2017.

LAW OF THE LAND

The exercise of judicial power rests with the courts of law and is completely independent of the executive and legislative branches. Judges of the lower courts, justices of the peace, are directly appointed by the grand duke. There are two branches of jurisdiction in Luxembourg: the judicial order and the administrative order. The administrative courts are designated by the constitution to deal with administrative- and finance-related cases. The judicial order has jurisdiction over minor cases in civil and commercial matters.

The coat of arms of Luxembourg was decided upon between 1235 and 1239 by Count Henry V with a design of cross bars of silver and blue, and a red lion rampant—rearing up on hind legs—crowned with gold. On June 23, both the National Day holiday and the grand duke's birthday are celebrated. Luxembourg's flag, with its three horizontal bands of red, white, and blue, is distinguishable from that of the Netherlands only by the shade of its blue—sky blue as opposed to the Dutch ultramarine blue.

The national anthem is the first and last verses of the song "Ons Hémecht" (ONS he-MECHT), "Our Motherland," composed in 1864 with words by Luxembourger Michel Lentz (1820–1893). Far from being a martial song, as with many countries, the Luxembourgish national anthem issues a vibrant appeal for peace.

> *O Thou above, whose powerful hand*
> *Makes States or lays them low,*
> *Protect this Luxembourger land*
> *From foreign yoke and woe.*
> *Your spirit of liberty bestow*
> *On us now as of yore.*
> *Let Freedom's sun in glory glow.*

A SMALL ARMY

Luxembourg has no compulsory military service, but as a NATO member, it has a contingent of soldiers recruited on a voluntary basis. Women serve in various positions in the military, with many taking on administrative jobs. After three years of active service, soldiers leave the army and are guaranteed jobs in the police force or postal service. A reserve force can be called up in times of international crisis. The army is under civilian control and the command of the grand duke.

The Constitutional Court ranks at the top of the judicial hierarchy. The court is composed of nine members and sits in Luxembourg City. It rules on the conformity of laws with the constitution, except for those laws approving treaties.

The jury system is not used in Luxembourg. Instead, there is a panel of an odd number of judges. A defendant is acquitted if a majority of the presiding judges finds him or her not guilty. A public prosecutor's department represents the state in the courts and acts under the authority of the minister of justice. Assisting them in their work is the police force, which is responsible for investigating crimes and delivering suspects to the courts, under the supervision of the attorney general.

INTERNET LINKS

http://www.bbc.com/news/world-europe-17548470
The BBC News country profile includes information about Luxembourg's leaders.

http://www.luxembourg.public.lu/en/le-grand-duche-se-presente/ systeme-politique/index.html
The official portal of Luxembourg explains the political system with many links to relevant content.

http://www.wort.lu/en/politics
Luxembourger Wort, an online news site, has a section devoted to politics.

http://www.wort.lu/en/luxembourg/luxembourg-s-royal-family-in-the-news-519cf128e4b038d84b4af619
The Wort also has a section of news stories about the royal family.

ECONOMY

luxembourg
meng stad · ma ville · my city

A banner promotes Luxembourg City as a destination for music, culture, and tourism.

4

The Grand Duchy is one of the world's top financial marketplaces. Some 150 international banks operate out of Luxembourg.

LUXEMBOURG IS A VERY PROSPEROUS country with a highly industrialized economy. Historically, this economy was built on steel, but today the financial sector leads the way, accounting for about 36 percent of economic production. Luxembourg enjoys one of the highest standards of living in the world. In 2016, its gross domestic product (GDP) *per capita* (per person) was $102,000, the second highest in the world, and the highest in Europe. (Tiny, affluent countries tend to lead the list—with oil-producing Qatar at the top in 2016—but for comparison, the GDP per capita that same year in the United States was $57,300 at number 18.)

Being such a small country, however, Luxembourg is highly dependent on foreign and cross-border workers to keep its economy running. These workers, mainly from France, Belgium, and Germany, account for about 39 percent of the labor force, and this huge block of nonresident workers skews the GDP per capita figure. While contributing to GDP, the cross-border workers are not considered part of the resident population

Gross domestic product (GDP) is a measure of a country's total production. The number reflects the total value of goods and services produced over a specific time period—typically one year. Economists use it to find out if a country's economy is growing or contracting. Growth is good, while a falling GDP means trouble. Dividing the GDP by the number of people in the country determines the GDP per capita. This number provides an indication of a country's average standard of living—the higher the better.

which is used to calculate the per capita statistic. In other words, the statistics have to be taken with a grain of salt, so to speak. If the foreign workers were counted in the per capita figure, the total would be significantly lower. That said, even if that adjustment were made, Luxembourg would still qualify as a wealthy country.

Salaries and wages are quite high, starting with the minimum wage. In 2015, an unskilled adult working a full-time job (forty hours a week) could count on a monthly gross income of 1,922.96 euros ($2,174.50); a skilled adult earned a minimum of 2,307.56 euros ($2,609.40) for the same number of hours. This is the highest minimum wage in Europe.

A SUCCESS STORY

The industry and commerce of Luxembourg profit from being centrally located in Europe. This has been exploited to good advantage. In the last century, the great transportation links with neighboring countries gave impetus to the steel industry, which helped propel Luxembourg to affluence. Steel from Luxembourg is used all over the world in the building of bridges, skyscrapers, and railways.

Liberal taxation laws as well as banking secrecy encouraged the rapid development of Luxembourg's financial sector. Social stability has brought the country considerable foreign investment and contributed to the public welfare, with unemployment remaining generally low. In 2016, the country's unemployment rate was 6.7 percent.

WORKFORCE

Luxembourg employs a large number of "cross-border" and foreign workers. Both lower- and higher-skilled labor is recruited, mostly from Belgium, Germany, and France. The country's unemployment rate is low compared with the rest of the European countries. The steady increase in employment has, however, slowed in the past few years.

The low unemployment rate is due mainly to a number of public measures enacted to combat unemployment, like early retirement plans and supported training projects for laid-off steel workers. Also, the government's policy of attracting new firms to settle in Luxembourg, especially in the banking and other service sectors, has been successful.

The economic development of Luxembourg over the last thirty years has been marked by a rapid change in the main types of employment. Focus has shifted to the services sector, such as banking, insurance, distributive trades, and communications. At the same time, manufacturing has been diversified.

Pedestrians walk through a busy shopping area in Luxembourg City.

SOCIAL CONSENSUS

One of the keys to the economic success story has been social consensus. To avoid conflicts among the many different nationalities in the country, it is often necessary to hammer out agreements. The close links that exist between the inhabitants of a small nation make it easier to find solutions on the basis of a national consensus. Although compromise usually costs everyone a little and never makes anyone entirely happy, it seems to have worked as a strategy.

Since the 1970s, economic problems have been dealt with by what is known as the Luxembourg Model. Consultation between the government and employees takes place on many different levels on committees and councils through a tripartite system, involving an official board made up of employer, trade union, and governmental representatives. Such a nonconfrontational approach to industrial relations and negotiations has so far sidestepped major disputes.

A general minimum wage to combat poverty has been in existence since 1945. All wage earners benefit from a salary scale whereby each increase of the level of prices leads to an automatic adjustment of salaries, pensions, and allowances. Thus the purchasing power of consumers is safeguarded.

AN EYE FOR OPPORTUNITIES

Luxembourgers have prospered by being quick to identify opportunities for their economy and to exploit market gaps. The banking service, in particular, is a good example. Luxembourg's freedom to maneuver as a tiny state inside the large EU is also important. It can attract business by offering special privileges that its larger neighbors will not or cannot give.

Equally important, Luxembourg has elected political leaders who know how to diversify a small economy by attracting investment and finding lucrative service industries, while preserving a good social climate. As a result, Luxembourg has, in recent decades, become a pioneer of the Eurobond market, a launchpad for the cable and satellite television business through the lure of deregulation, and a prime personal finance center with customized

The European Investment Bank, informally known as "the Bank of the European Union," is the EU's nonprofit long-term lending institution. Based in Luxembourg, it finances a broad spectrum of projects, from major infrastructure to small businesses, as long as they further European integration. Its role is bringing people closer together, stimulating trade, and building up links between Europe's regions, while also observing the rules of rigorous banking practice.

It has lent money at a low-interest fixed-rate, for major road, highway, and rail links, and for air transportation and telecommunications systems across Europe. There has also been funding for advanced technology, such as aeronautical engineering. A large amount of money is funneled into environmental protection, like waste and sewage treatment plants. Last are the important energy projects, particularly those that are developing alternative sources of energy, like wind farms.

The European Investment Bank maintains a very sound capital base and funds its lending through bond issues.

banking services and tax-efficient investment. Major international concerns have established new subsidiaries or expanding existing plants. Luxembourg is host to an array of Euro institutions, including the European Court of Justice, the European Investment Bank, the Court of Auditors, the administrative center of the European Parliament, and other lucrative earners and spenders clustered together in the popular capital city.

BANKING AND FINANCIAL SERVICES

Among the main reasons for the growth of Luxembourg as a financial center, apart from the linguistic abilities of Luxembourgers, are the laws concerning taxation. Luxembourg does not tax the interest earned in foreigners' accounts and has strict rules of banking secrecy.

For thousands of wealthy Europeans, who prefered not to pay taxes on their money at their own country's top rates, it was a pleasant outing to drive to Luxembourg and have a good lunch after depositing funds in a bank. This was simpler than a trip to the Cayman Islands, for example, though now, of course, it can all be accomplished electronically. Luxembourg is a safe financial bet because it's part of a single market with the euro as its currency. No taxation is the first wall of the fortress. The inner wall is banking secrecy.

The Banque et Caisse d'Epargne de l'Etat, the state-owned bank, is the most famous bank building in Luxembourg.

While banks are obliged to check the origin of funds, they are not compelled to disclose such information, except when judicial procedures have been initiated. In addition, all countries other than Luxembourg impose controls on the ability of banks to generate profit.

These practices, which give Luxembourg its reputation as a tax haven, have prompted other EU countries to try to introduce European legislation to end such tax advantages. The Bank of Credit and Commerce International, based in Luxembourg, was shut down in 1991 by international regulators who believed it was involved in illegal activities. Any moves to change the laws, however, have always been successfully blocked by Luxembourg, whose revenues depend heavily on the ongoing profitability of its banks.

LUXLEAKS SCANDAL

It's no secret that Luxembourg has long been considered a tax haven. As such, it has benefited economically but at the same time acquired a shady reputation. In 2009, the Organization for Economic Cooperation and

A tax haven is an unofficial term with an uncertain definition. Generally, it's a country that offers foreign individuals and businesses a safe place to keep their money while having to pay minimal or no taxes. Secrecy is an important piece of the arrangement. Banks in a tax haven country are not required to disclose much, if any, of their clients' financial

information to foreign tax authorities. A tax haven does not require individual clients to live in the country, nor do businesses have to operate out of the country, in order to benefit from the local tax policies.

Tax havens, therefore, provide corporations and wealthy individuals with a way to avoid paying taxes at home. The secrecy aspect also attracts the illegal profits of criminal enterprises of all sorts, including money laundering and terrorist financing. The danger is compounded when the interests of the financial services sector and its clients exert a powerful influence over the country's government, which leads directly to corruption.

Development (OECD) identified Luxembourg on its "gray list" as a country that had not implemented necessary "internationally agreed tax standards." Alarmed, Luxembourgish officials quickly signed some agreements designed to improve transparency and cooperation in the banking industry. Doing so got the Grand Duchy off the "bad guys" list, but its problems weren't over.

In 2014, an investigation by the International Consortium of Investigative Journalists exposed confidential tax rulings in Luxembourg involving more than three hundred multinational corporations. The leaked documents revealed that the government had helped corporations such as Microsoft, Disney, and Koch Industries avoid billions of dollars in taxes to their home-base countries.

The resulting scandal, which came to be called Luxembourg Leaks, or LuxLeaks, undermined Luxembourg's reputation in the minds of the public, and focused international criticism on Luxembourg's then-prime minister, Jean-Claude Junker. It also prompted European Commission investigations into the legality of some of these tax-avoidance schemes. Tax dodging by multinationals costs the EU countries 50 billion to 70 billion euros in lost tax revenues every year.

Meanwhile, the government of Luxembourg spearheaded a new branding effort to promote a positive image for the country and improve its international standing.

INDUSTRY

Industry, including mining, manufacturing, and construction, is the other primary sector of the economy. Iron and steel once were the dominant forces in the economy—from the late nineteenth century until the crippling steel industry crisis in 1975. That industry has, nonetheless, now been completely restructured, albeit with major cutbacks in jobs.

In 2002, the nation's steel company, ARBED, merged with the Spanish company Aceralia and the French company Usinor to form Arcelor. In 2006, the company again merged, with the world's then largest steelmaker, Mittal, forming today's largest steel producer, ArcelorMittal.

Based in Luxembourg, the company is multinational in scope. In 2013, it employed more than 232,000 people worldwide. ArcelorMittal is also the Grand Duchy's largest private employer, with some 4,600 Luxembourgish employees in 2014. Iron and steel remain the country's main industry, despite dwindling iron resources and reduced demand for Luxembourg's steel exports.

Since the 1970s, the Grand Duchy has been working to diversify its economy, and rely less on steel. Today, Luxembourg's industries include

IRON IN THE FIRE

The Celts and Romans first mastered the production of iron about 1000 BCE. But it was not until the 1850s that the Luxembourgish horizon became lined with blast furnace stacks spewing out clouds of rust-colored fumes. The development of the iron industry brought affluence to the country, and villages changed into towns.

The reign of iron lasted for more than a century, until 1975 and the onset of the world crisis in the iron and steel industry. Mining activities wound down, coming to a standstill in the early 1980s. Now many of the mining galleries have been turned into museums.

chemicals, plastic and synthetic materials, mechanical engineering, the automotive industry, precision instrument engineering, electronic delivery services, glass, and wood.

AGRICULTURE

The agricultural industry, which includes forestry and fishing, has continued to decline in economic importance since the beginning of industrialization in the early nineteenth century. Luxembourg's agricultural industry's share of the GDP fell from 4 percent in 1980 to 2 percent in 1985 and 0.6 percent in 2001. In 2016, it contributed only 0.2 percent to the national income.

About 50 percent of land use in Luxembourg is for agricultural purposes, and another 33.5 percent is forest. The principal crops are grains, potatoes, and wine grapes. Substantial numbers of cattle, pigs, and poultry are also raised. The amount of land committed to forestry has actually increased over the years, and the cultivation of the main types of trees, coniferous and broad-leaved, has also increased.

Some 1 percent of the land is used for grapevine growing. The valley of the Moselle River enjoys a mild climate and ideal soil, lime, and clay, all which make this region highly suited for producing white wines. It is very similar to the Champagne region of France.

Luxembourg's wine industry rests on two keystones. First is the establishment of six cooperative cellars between 1921 and 1948. All of these producers have now combined under an umbrella organization to improve production. For example, the merged vineyard slopes are now efficiently cultivated, compared with what could be done with the former small and irregular parcels of land.

Second, a national wine label stamped on every bottle by the state institution of viticulture guarantees the authenticity and quality of the wines. This national mark acts both as a stimulus to wine producers to create wines of ever higher quality and offers consumers a guarantee that they are getting a first-class wine.

A view of agricultural land in Luxembourg.

TOURISM

The spectacular forests and river valleys of Luxembourg are unmatched, in such a small area, anywhere else in Europe. It is the variety of landscape, combined with castles, picturesque market towns, sunny vineyards, varied cuisines, and archaeological remains that has fostered the tourist industry.

Being a small, landlocked country, Luxembourg naturally can't compete for the tourist looking for beaches and seashore. However, in 2015, tourism contributed around 5.3 million euros (about $5 million) to the country's GDP and directly employed around eight thousand people. Business tourism is a particularly strong component, as Luxembourg City, in particular, offers a very competitive environment for corporate and professional conventions and conferences. It provides a multilingual urban setting with excellent transportation, hotels, restaurants, and cultural events.

Luxembourg's proximity to other European nations also makes it an attractive destination for visitors wishing to tour several countries while on their vacation.

INTERNET LINKS

https://www.icij.org/project/luxembourg-leaks
The International Consortium of Investigative Journalists offers an in-depth explanation of LuxLeaks.

http://www.luxembourg.public.lu/en/le-grand-duche-se-presente/systeme-politique/concertation/modele-social/index.html
This site provides a good overview of the Luxembourg Social Model.

https://www.nytimes.com/2015/11/24/business/international/luxembourg-goes-in-for-an-image-makeover.html
This *New York Times* article discusses Luxembourg's attempt to improve its reputation.

ENVIRONMENT

A traffic light for cyclists signals a pedestrian crossing.

I N THE 2016 ENVIRONMENTAL performance index, which ranks countries' performance on high-priority environmental issues, Luxembourg came in at number 20 out of 180. The top spot went to Finland—in fact, the top four countries were in Scandinavia. The listing, determined annually by Yale University's Center for Environmental Law & Policy and other groups, evaluates each country's air quality, water resources, sanitation, biodiversity and habitat, climate and energy, and other data. Luxembourg's score indicates the country is doing very well in its environmental performance, but that there's room to improve.

5

Luxembourg hosts around two hundred green technology companies, working in renewable energy, waste management, water, and eco-construction. These private businesses are supported in their work by twenty-eight public-sector agencies and six research institutes, including the University of Luxembourg.

A public trash bin encourages cleanliness in Kirchberg.

Like most European countries, Luxembourg has not escaped air and water pollution in urban areas, but as a member of the European Union (EU), the nation participates in European initiatives to protect the environment. The EU Environment Council is responsible for ensuring that the environmental perspective is given proper consideration in international projects and economic activities and at all levels of government. The council is formed of EU ministers for the environment, and meetings are held formally four times a year and informally twice more a year.

WASTE MANAGEMENT

Luxembourgers generates one of the highest annual amounts of municipal solid waste (SMW) in Europe—about 1,459 pounds per person (662 kg/person) in 2012. But also has one of the highest rates of separately collected MSW.

An extensive framework of laws and regulations govern Luxembourg's waste management. These policies initially focused on disposal but now emphasize recovery and reduction, and define a waste-management hierarchy. Waste is classified into five separate categories—household, industrial, inert, hospital, and sewage. The strategy for managing waste is to recover and reuse as much as possible. As a result, mobile and permanent collection sites can be found all over the country. Separate collection bins are allocated to paper, glass, bulky items, and organic waste, as well as recoverable metal and plastic items.

BIODIVERSITY

Despite its small size, Luxembourg is home to a fairly wide range of species and habitats. As in most countries, however, human activities such as

agriculture, urbanization, transportation, and tourism are increasingly impacting the countryside in general and many natural or seminatural ecosystems in particular.

A family of European badgers.

Out of fifty-one species of mammals, about 2 percent are threatened, and another 10 percent are near threatened. The otter has disappeared from the rivers; populations of the badger, on the other hand, which were decimated by gassing during a period of rabies control, have been restored. The wildcat is still present in the Ardennes and in abandoned open-pit mines in the south.

There are 296 bird species (though statistics vary by source). Several species, such as the marsh harrier, the peregrine falcon, the black grouse, the hoopoe, the crested lark, and the tawny pipit, disappeared in the 1960s. The black stork has reappeared and is nesting in the Belgian and Luxembourgish plateau of the Ardennes.

Small game hunting is permitted, though the number of species classified as game by law is few. Game hunting for larger animals such as stags, roe deer, and wild boar, which depend on forest habitat, is on the increase.

The Schiessentümpel waterfall cascades under a stone bridge on the Black Ernz River in the Mullerthal region of Luxembourg.

LAND AND WATER HABITAT

Forest covers approximately 35 percent of the country. The Ardennes region is the most heavily forested area. Beech and oak are the most common trees found in much of the forestland, though there are other types of woods that attract attention for their rarity and for the flora and fauna found in them. These include ravine forests of maple, pine, swampy alder stands, and peaty birch woods. Luxembourg's forests are made accessible by the public road network and are open to the public.

CLIMATE CHANGE

Climate change is a serious problem for the earth, with significant effects already taking place. The average global temperature has risen more than 1 degree Celsius (1.8 degrees Fahrenheit). Global sea level rose about 8 inches (20.3 cm) in the last century—but the

rate in the last two decades is nearly double that of the last century. Ocean temperatures are rising and the waters are becoming more acidic, polar ice masses are melting, and the number of extreme weather events is increasing. The vast majority of scientists agree that global warming is occurring at an unprecedented rate and the primary cause is the greenhouse gases emitted by human activities.

World leaders recognize that no one country can address the problem of climate change on its own. The Kyoto Protocol, named after the Japanese town of Kyoto where the 1997 treaty was written, was an attempt for countries to work together to tackle the issue of climate change by agreeing to reduce their carbon dioxide emissions. Now, some twenty years on, the results of the protocol are mixed. Although many participants went above and beyond their targeted goals, some of the world's largest countries—and largest emitters, including the United States—did not get on board. As a member state of the EU, Luxembourg is a party to the Kyoto agreement.

In 2015, a new attempt was developed to address the problem internationally, and the EU was a major driver of the effort. In December 2015, 195 countries adopted the first-ever universal, legally binding global climate deal. The Paris Agreement, within the United Nations Framework Convention on Climate Change (UNFCCC), sets out a global action plan to put the world on track to avoid dangerous climate change by limiting global warming to well below 2°C (35.6 f). EU leaders have set three key targets for the year 2030:

- *at least 40 percent cuts in greenhouse gas emissions (from 1990 levels),*
- *at least 27 percent share for renewable energy, and*
- *at least 27 percent improvement in energy efficiency.*

The Moselle River flows past the village of Wormeldange.

Apart from the Chiers River, which flows toward France and forms part of the Meuse basin, all the rivers are part of the Moselle subbasin, which empties into the Rhine River. While the density of the rivers and streams is highest in the narrow valleys of the Ardennes, the rivers and streams in Gutland in the south wind mostly through agricultural valleys.

PROTECTING THE ENVIRONMENT

The Water and Forest Administration has been in charge of nature conservation since 1965. The 1965 Nature Protection Act was passed to protect landscapes and the rural environment. It reflected an emerging awareness of the negative impact of uncontrolled building development on city outskirts and the urbanization of the countryside. The farsighted act was amended three times, in 1978, 1982, and in 1992.

The objectives of the act are to conserve the natural environment by protecting and restoring natural areas and landscapes; to protect flora and

FREE COMPOST FOR RUBBISH

Luxembourg was one of the first European countries to split up rubbish into three kinds: organic, plastics, and general. Recycling bins for batteries, medicines, and clothing, as well as the usual glass and paper, are common.

One innovative and popular recycling measure is free compost made from local garbage. Residents can visit the nearest local commercial compost dump and obtain free compost for a garden or balcony. The compost is produced from that residential area's garbage, so, in essence, residents are getting back their own garbage but in a useful form.

fauna, and their biotopes—their natural regions; to maintain and improve biological balances; to protect natural resources from damage of all kinds; and to improve the structures of the natural environment.

Several nongovernmental organizations (NGOs) are also actively involved in protecting species through specific programs. The oldest association is the LNVL or the National League for the Protection of Nature and Birds. Other associations indirectly involved in environmental management include the Luxembourg Hunting Federation, the Saint Hubert Club, the Luxembourg Anglers' Federation, and the Luxembourg Naturalists' Society. The latter is actively engaged in research and has close links with the Natural History Museum.

INTERNET LINKS

http://epi.yale.edu/country/luxembourg
The Environmental Performance Index indicators for Luxembourg are found on this site.

https://ec.europa.eu/clima/index_en
The European Commission Climate Action site details the EU's efforts to address climate change.

LUXEMBOURGERS

People of various nationalities reflect the international flavor of Luxembourg City at a farmer's market in Place Guillaume II square.

6

ETHNIC LUXEMBOURGERS ARE mainly of Germanic origin, descending from the Franks, a tribe that lived in Northern Europe many centuries ago. These people make up the majority of Luxembourgers, but just barely. The grand duchy is a multicultural nation. In some ways, it has become something of a microcosm of the world, especially of Europe. Since the beginning of its industrialization, Luxembourg has sustained a strong growth in population. This is because of continuous immigration since the end of the nineteenth century. In 1990 Luxembourg had a population of about 200,000. In 2016, this number had nearly tripled to 582,291.

POPULATION TRENDS

In spite of the conspicuous total growth, the overall trend nowadays is a falling birth rate. The population growth that has occurred over the last forty years or so has come about because of immigrants.

Immigrants make up a significant percent of the population—46.7 percent in 2016. In percentage terms, there are more foreigners in Luxembourg than in any other country in the European Union. Despite this large newcomer presence, there are few problems arising from this, and the population lives well in multicultural coexistence. Nevertheless, as the number of foreigners nears the 50 percent mark, and many don't speak any of the three Luxembourg official languages, some discomfort can be seen among the native population.

Flags bedeck the streets for National Day in June.

NATIONAL PRIDE

Luxembourgers are the result of the merging of two quite distinct cultures: in the west is the French group to which Luxembourg is linked by its civilization, and in the east is the Germanic group to which the country belongs linguistically. From the end of the third century, migrations of Germanic tribes began settling in the region of Luxembourg. All this resulted in a national character based on its ability to enrich itself from other cultures and a genuine desire to mix foreign contributions with its own heritage.

Citizens do not fear losing their Luxembourgish identity because they see themselves as completely different from both the Germans and the French. Repeatedly invaded, they have survived, and that has bred their tremendous loyalty. This innate pride and patriotism is easily noticeable today. Delighted to discover the role their nation can play on an international level, as part of a wider Europe, Luxembourgers have gained confidence in their ability as a nation.

CHARACTER AND PERSONALITY

Luxembourgers are known as a friendly, convivial, polite, and open-minded people who have a well-developed sense of hospitality. Many older Luxembourgers are particularly friendly toward visitors from the United States because of the pivotal role American soldiers played in the liberation of their country from the Nazis.

People enjoy a warm day outdoors in the center of Luxembourg City.

Some regional differences are observed, however. People in the southern part of Luxembourg have a reputation for being outspoken. In the north, Luxembourgers are said to have developed an easygoing joie de vivre because their harsh living conditions have led the locals to take advantage of life's enjoyments as best as they can.

Cautious, hardworking, practical, conservative, and traditional: these are traits often associated with the Luxembourger. In addition, Luxembourgish entrepreneurs are known for their characteristic self-composure in most situations.

Enjoying the pleasures of life, however, is as important to them as work, and with their passion for festivities, Luxembourgers grasp opportunities to celebrate and to organize parades and processions. The national motto, seen carved in stone walls, perhaps best sums up the people's character: "We want to remain what we are."

MELTING POT

In terms of ethnic composition, the greatest groups of immigrants in Luxembourg are Portuguese, Italian, French, Belgian, and German. In recent years, however, refugees from war-torn areas of the Middle East and Africa have found their way to the little country.

The Luxembourgers' ability to compromise can be seen by the successive waves of immigration and the smooth integration of guest workers: Italians in 1870s and the 1920s for the steel industry, and the present surge of Portuguese, which began in the 1960s, especially active in building and construction. A generally positive attitude toward immigrants willing to integrate and pursue culturally similar values has produced a melting pot without threatening national identity. The annual Festival of Immigration attracts the patronage of the highest dignitaries, and the major political parties all emphasize the importance to the country of the presence of nonindigenous people.

In Luxembourg, despite the many different nationalities, there has been little, if any, intolerance or racial unrest. Any fascist notion is fiercely rejected, because during World War II Luxembourg suffered greatly at the hands of Nazi zealots and the losses were painfully extensive. Hardly a family has not lost some member in the German concentration camps, on the Russian front, or in the Resistance movement.

An important factor that undoubtedly eases integration is the country's low unemployment rate. Social unrest and conflict are less likely to occur where jobs are plentiful and individuals have some control over their destiny.

The problems faced by immigrants are more often of a practical nature, such as housing shortages and language barriers, which hamper many from getting ahead, than overt racism. A young man from Cape Verde who works and lives in Luxembourg and is married to a local woman, says he experiences no difficulty with the fact that he is black and she white. "Everyone is so friendly to me." The disturbing trend toward a "new poverty" among illegal immigrants living in the country is a far greater threat than prejudice.

DRESS

Today it is difficult to find traditional Luxembourgish dress worn just anywhere, for it is likely to be seen only on festive occasions. Women's customary, time-honored dress consists of a full-length royal blue skirt, gathered at the waist, and trimmed with a white border above the hem. Worn over this is a small, semicircular white apron, richly embroidered at the bottom. A long-sleeved, plain white cotton blouse, a red or white cloth bonnet, and a red cloth shawl across the shoulders complete the outfit. Flat black shoes and thick white stockings are worn, and a wicker basket is typically carried. When a dance routine, an intrinsic part of the culture for women, is performed, the usual dress is a white blouse with a short black skirt.

Men's traditional dress is a blue tunic in a smock style with a red edging. Black knee-length breeches are worn, together with a white shirt and either a black bow tie or a red scarf. Knee-high socks, black shoes with silver buckles, and a peaked cap finish off the outfit.

For men living in the rural parts of the country and earning their living as farmers, the usual festive costume is a red scarf and short blue overalls.

INTERNET LINKS

http://www.luxembourg.public.lu/en/le-grand-duche-se-presente/luxembourg-tour-horizon/population-et-multiculturalite/index.html
This page presents demographic statistics for Luxembourg.

http://www.politico.eu/article/luxembourg-migration-crisis-eu-asylum-refugees
This 2015 article takes a close look at Luxembourg's attitude toward immigrants and refugees.

LIFESTYLE

The setting sun reflects golden light in Luxembourg City.

7

THE OVERWHELMING MAJORITY OF Luxembourgers, 90 percent, live in cities or towns, rather than in the countryside. Luxembourgish society is both urban and very cosmopolitan, a finding that can sometimes seem at odds with the fact that most of the country's land is used for agriculture.

A pedestrian thoroughfare encourages shoppers on a downtown street.

In a rarely seen phenomenon, a 2012 study found that women in Luxembourg earned about 3 percent more money than men. The average annual salary for women that year was 45,767 euros (app. $58,582 at the average exchange rate for 2012), compared to 44,224 euros ($56,607) for men.

Although Luxembourg is a small nation, it is not overcrowded. Luxembourgers have ample access to their own space. The pace of life in the capital city can be fast and stressful at times, like any other European capital. Away from the city, though, life is slower and more laid-back.

STANDARD OF LIVING

Luxembourg has the highest standard of living in the EU. Numerous indicators confirm its prosperity. Citizens of the grand duchy receive more social benefits per one thousand inhabitants than anywhere else in Europe. When prices go up, wages and pensions increase accordingly, so consumers do not feel the pinch.

Only Germany has more cars, Denmark more telephones, and the Netherlands more hospitals, per capita. Some 70 percent of Luxembourgers own their homes, and housing standards are high, with all having electricity and running water. Luxembourg has the highest per capita consumption of electricity in Europe.

Factors that contribute to the high quality of life in Luxembourg are an ideal population density and the absence of big cities. Short distances to and from work, combined with adequate transportation facilities, also help make daily life easier.

HEARTH AND HOME

Nearly two-thirds of the total population of Luxembourg lives in the ten major towns, which are also centers of industrial production. About 30 percent of Luxembourgers live in just three of these towns. Luxembourg City, the capital, alone has more than 110,000 inhabitants, out of which Luxembourgers themselves account for only three out ten residents. Because

Buses and cars pass by baroque style buildings in the grand duchy's main city.

of exorbitant rents, the center of Luxembourg City sees little activity outside of business hours. Instead, residential neighborhoods have sprung up in the vicinity of the city, neatly separated from industrial areas.

In Luxembourg, as in the rest of Europe, the number of people living in rural areas is fast dwindling. Preserving the rural heritage is a difficult task and the delicate balance between town and country is in some peril. Although the countryside offers abundant recreational activities, some rural areas are unable to sustain the level of commerce necessary for a dynamic local community. Infrastructure is often poor and services inadequate compared with urban areas.

The average Luxembourgish family has a detached two- to three-bedroom house. All have central heating, predominantly by oil, have double-glazed windows, and usually include such features as marble counters and wooden parquet floors. Gardens and flowers are important to Luxembourgers. For people without a garden, colorful window boxes are the next best thing.

Larochette, a village in the Mullerthal region, is well-known for its surrounding forests and medieval ruins.

For a predominantly Roman Catholic country, the marriage of Xavier Bettel to Gauthier Destenay in May 2015 was a remarkable sign of shifting attitudes. Bettel was, after all, the prime minister of Luxembourg. Less than a year after the Grand Duchy legalized same-sex marriage, the prime minister married his long-time partner. The civil ceremony was private, but the news was public. Bettel, who served as the mayor of Luxembourg City prior to becoming prime minister, had publicly acknowledged his sexual orientation in 2008. However, he has never made a big deal of it and has said being gay is not central to his political life.

Prime Minister Xavier Bettel, right, and his husband Gauthier Destenay.

Bettel is not the first openly gay world leader, but he is the first EU leader, and the second head of government (after Iceland's Prime Minister Jóhanna Sigurðardóttir in 2010) to marry someone of the same sex while in office.

Public and political sentiment toward same-sex marriage in Luxembourg shifted over a very short period of time. In 2006, a poll found that 58 percent of Luxembourgers supported same-sex marriage. Another poll in 2013 found 83 percent support for it. Political opinion reflected the same change. In 2007, a motion calling for the legalization of same-sex marriage was rejected by the parliament, on a 38–22 vote. In 2014, the bill passed in a 56–4 vote.

FAMILY VALUES

Luxembourgers have strong traditional values. Families are very important to most people and are woven into a significant part of the social fabric. Boarding schools are quite rare, and every opportunity is taken to spend time with the family—even lunch breaks.

Still, changes are taking place, even in small towns and villages where conservatism and a reluctance to change is often entrenched. As women become more active in the working life, many are delaying marriage and childbearing. This is a fundamental social change, which neighboring countries have experienced for a much longer time.

WOMEN

Women account for about 44 percent of the working population in Luxembourg. They largely dominate the health and social work sector, education, real estate, and domestic workers employed by householders. The motivation for working is usually to provide a higher standard of living for her family. A growing proportion of women now bring in at least half the household income.

The average age of women having their first baby is 30.2 years, which is, comparatively, one of the oldest in the world. This statistic corresponds with the tendency of women in more affluent, industrialized societies to start their families later, usually after devoting years to their education and careers. The rise of working mothers is reflected in the increase in childcare facilities. In 2012, a survey found that 58 percent of families in the Grand Duchy used some type of child care. The number of childcare facilities has grown enormously in recent years—from 7,700 spots available for children to about 46,000 places in 2013.

With the growing dominance of the service industries, more job opportunities have been created for women. Nonetheless, women remain underrepresented in industry and the professions, despite laws that ensure equal access to employment and equal pay, training, and working conditions.

PARENTAL LEAVE

Like many European countries, Luxembourg's support for families with young children is quite generous. In 2016, Luxembourg's parliament approved a new parental leave law which provides for more flexibility than was previously available for parents of newborns and young children. Parents, both mothers and fathers, can now elect to take leave from their jobs for

- *four or six months' full-time leave;*
- *eight or twelve months part-time leave;*
- *one day of parental leave per week for twenty months; or*
- *four individual months of parental leave within twenty months.*

Mothers and fathers can now take parental leave simultaneously. In the past, they had to take it at different times. In addition, families receive an income from the government which is the equivalent to Luxembourg's minimum wage. This works out to nearly 2,000 euros (which is approximately the same amount in dollars in 2017) per month per parent, for a maximum of 3,204 euros a month. This income is in lieu of a full time job, and as such, is still subject to taxes and other withholding amounts.

YOUNG PEOPLE

According to the 2011 census, young people under age twenty represent almost a quarter (23.3 percent) of Luxembourg's population. Almost half of them (43.7 percent) are not Luxembourg nationals. A major worry facing these young people—and this is not unique to Luxembourg—is jobs and careers. In July 2013, 18 percent of people under the age of twenty-five were unemployed.

Youth centers in Luxembourg, often called *maisons des jeunes* provide a range of daytime and evening activities, mainly for teenagers, usually young males. Typical organized activities include audiovisual initiatives that allow young people to make films about their communities, and training on the use of the Internet.

EDUCATION

Primary education begins at age six and lasts for six years. At age twelve, after taking entrance exams, pupils are assigned to one of three types of secondary schools: grammar (college prep), secondary technical, or complementary education. Each of these has a different curriculum and vocational objectives. Education is compulsory for all until the age of fifteen.

Students attending grammar school who are successful in the final examination at the age of eighteen or nineteen can choose to go on to university studies. Since 2003, Luxembourg has had its own public, research-oriented university, the University of Luxembourg, with three campuses. Courses are usually held in two languages—French/English, French/German, or English/German. Luxembourgers who want to go abroad to study may, of course, still do so.

The colorful Athenee de Luxembourg is a high school in the capital city.

In the secondary technical system, a student may stay until age eighteen, leaving with a vocational qualification, an apprenticeship, or a diploma for higher technical studies.

The complementary education course is for students who fail to get into either of the mainstream options. Complementary education classes have come under considerable criticism because they offer poor chances for gaining qualifications and are attended by low achievers, many of whom are young immigrants with inadequate preparation.

Children with physical disabilities receive special education, separate from the mainstream. Many parents disagree with this practice, believing that their disabled child would benefit from being schooled alongside the able-bodied.

Luxembourg provides an extensive vocational guidance service. It starts in primary school and continues throughout the transition from school to occupational life and remains available to adults in their later years. The service caters to all age groups, though it concentrates on those just leaving school. Young people often benefit from counseling to find employment, and this is the original concept behind having such a service in the educational system.

THE WELFARE STATE

The average life expectancy at birth has risen from 50 years in 1900 to 82.3 years in 2016—79.8 years for males, and 84.9 years for females—one of the highest in the world. The birth rate was about 11.4 per 1,000 Luxembourgers in 2016, which is relatively low. The result is a growing number of elderly people but fewer people of working age to provide for them. About 15 percent of Luxembourgers are 65 years old or older.

Economic consequences include increases to the state burden of old-age pensions and sickness benefits. Political consequences arise from finding the money to pay for these growing costs. Thus far, welfare policy in Luxembourg has withstood attempts to cut benefits. Clearly, any move to do so would be very unpopular with the voters.

Social policies are highly developed. All types of employment are subject to compulsory contributory benefits, which is a combination of taxes paid by employees and employers. The resulting comprehensive social insurance plan covers medical and hospital treatments, disability and old-age pensions, family allowances, and unemployment benefits. A major advantage of this system is that everyone receives health-care benefits, unlike in the United States, where basically only the aged and the poor receive governmental help. Hospital treatment is free, but those who can afford better attention from private physicians or hospitals, for example, experience less time waiting for an operation and are free to buy private medical insurance. The numbers of general physicians, specialists, and available hospital beds have all increased substantially during the last decade.

The family allowance, which most industrialized countries have, with the notable exception of the United States, is a universal cash benefit that goes to every family regardless of income. The government itself does not administer social services. Social services are run by public bodies made up of representatives of the government, employers, and employees.

INTERNET LINKS

http://www.luxembourg.public.lu/en/vivre/famille/index.html
The Grand Duchy's official portal offers a section on family life.

http://www.en.uni.lu
This is the University of Luxembourg website in English.

http://www.wort.lu/en/luxembourg/a-short-history-of-women-s-rights-achievements-in-luxembourg-51347125e4b0bae312230b07
The *Luxembourger Wort* presents a timeline of women's progress in the duchy.

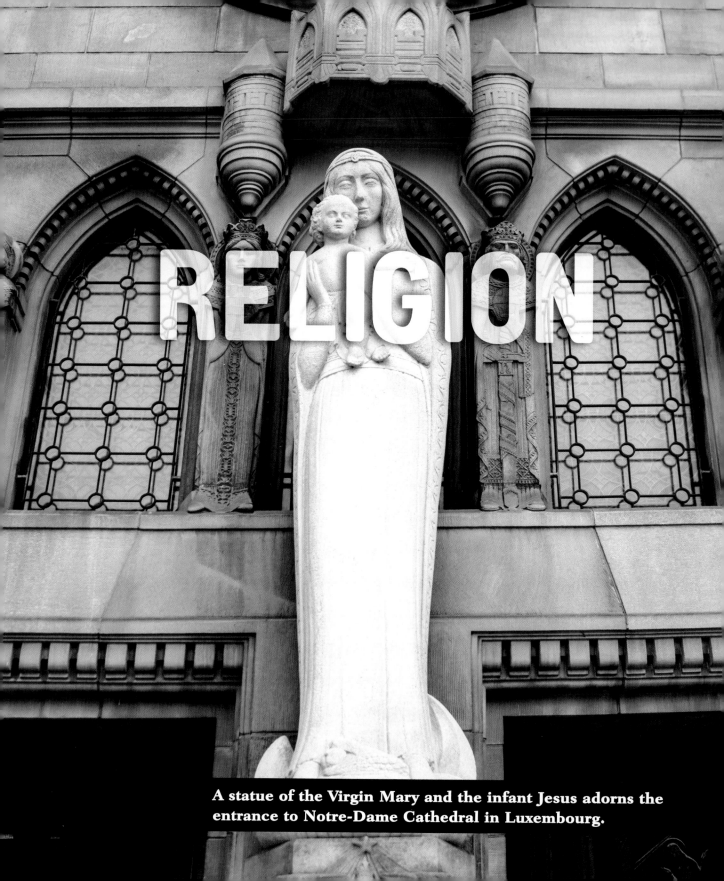

RELIGION

A statue of the Virgin Mary and the infant Jesus adorns the entrance to Notre-Dame Cathedral in Luxembourg.

8

LIKE MOST OF EUROPE, LUXEMBOURG is predominantly Christian. As is also true in much of the continent, more and more people now identify themselves as nonpracticing, nonreligious, or atheist. This recent trend is illustrated in the comparative results of the European Values Study. In 1999, 22 percent of Luxembourgish respondents said they went to church "at least once a week," whereas in 2008, only a mere 3 percent did so; in 1999, 35 percent attended church "occasionally" versus 24 percent in 2008; and in 1999, 33 percent said they "never" went to church, but in 2008, nonattendance had grown to 37 percent. Nevertheless, most Luxembourgers themselves as Roman Catholics, at least in terms of their culture and heritage.

Determining the demographics of religious participation in Luxembourg depends on nongovernmental surveys. Since 1979, the law prohibits any question about religion in population censuses.

In the past, religion was as divisive an issue in Luxembourg as in the rest of Europe. Many battles and massacres took place in the name of religion. Today, over 95 percent of Luxembourgers are Roman Catholic. Any discrimination on the basis of religion is illegal. Luxembourgers remain deeply committed to Catholicism, and their religion is still an important part of their cultural life.

FROM DRUIDISM TO CHRISTIANITY

The Druids were an ancient priestly order who ruled in this area until Roman law, and later Christianity, put an end to their dominance. Little is known about the Druids other than that they were part of complex culture. They venerated numerous gods and natural objects, such as trees and water, and practiced magical rituals. Assemblies were held in consecrated spots, such as groves of oaks. Mistletoe growing on these oaks was sacred and used in medicine.

The Basilica of Saint Willibrord, a Benedictine monastery in Echternach, is a popular tourist attraction, particularly for its hopping procession.

Christianity was introduced early in Luxembourg, during the third century, but only began to flourish in the seventh century with the arrival of Irish and English missionaries. The Anglo-Saxon priest Saint Willibrord (c. 658—739) converted all of the Low Countries to Christianity. He worked for many years from Echternach, in eastern Luxembourg, from which he spread the message of Catholicism throughout the region. Saint Willibrord was buried in Echternach, where his crypt became one of the most important pilgrimage destinations in the region. Many faithful believed the aura around the altar of the crypt could cure plague, leprosy, and eye afflictions.

A MEDIEVAL CENTER

During the Middle Ages (fifth to fifteen centuries), learning was concentrated in large monastic centers, where monks preserved important books by carefully copying them, often adding elaborate illustrations. Most of this work of copying was concentrated on the gospels, which are the story of Christ's life and teaching as told in the New Testament of the Bible.

One of the most important monastic centers during the early Middle Ages was Echternach. The center is remembered today chiefly for the Echternach Gospels, lavishly decorated eleventh-century manuscripts that are some of the best and most treasured examples of medieval manuscript illumination.

The old Benedictine abbey that still stands in Echternach was founded in the seventh century by Saint Willibrord. Known as the Basilica, it has four wings of 230 feet (70 m) each built around a large square courtyard. One of the most important religious buildings in the country, it enshrines a magnificent white sarcophagus holding the remains of Saint Willibrord. The Basilica was partially destroyed during the Battle of the Bulge in 1944, but has now been completely restored.

The lion, a symbol of St. Mark, is an example of an illustrated page from the Echternach Gospels.

THE PROTESTANT CHALLENGE

During the Middle Ages, all of Europe was Roman Catholic. But with the spread of the Reformation in the late fifteenth and early sixteenth centuries, Protestant beliefs and practices began to spread and slowly dominate. The Reformation, an attempt to reform the Catholic Church, was begun by Martin Luther in 1517. Luther's attacks on issues of doctrine, and the widespread corruption in the Catholic Church hierarchy, changed religious practices in Europe. Many breakaway sects grew rapidly and took up revolutionary views, particularly a militant Protestantism called Calvinism.

The Spanish, however, who ruled the Low Countries at that time, were staunch defenders of the Catholic faith. That was also the time of the brutal Inquisition in Spain, when no torture was too terrible to inflict upon dissenters. Widespread resentment at the Spaniards' attempt to hold their subjects submissive to the Roman Catholic Church grew as Protestantism became firmly entrenched elsewhere.

Religious differences flared up between the north and south of the Low Countries when the south (present-day Luxembourg and Belgium) became alarmed at the spread of Lutheranism and Calvinism. The new Protestant doctrines failed to penetrate Luxembourg's borders, which remained Catholic and loyal to Spain. The north, today's Netherlands, became Protestant. All over Europe, rulers had to decide whether to accept or reject this new Christian religion, and this split between Catholicism and Protestantism ravaged Europe for more than a century.

RELIGION TODAY

Today the population is still overwhelmingly Roman Catholic. When the pope visited the country in 1985, the bishop was elevated to archbishop and placed under the direct authority of the pope without any intermediate hierarchy, a position usually reserved for cardinals. That was an almost unprecedented occurrence, an illustration of how important Luxembourg is to the Roman Catholic Church.

Almost all Protestant churches are represented in Luxembourg, though their influence is small. The evangelicals—believers in the absolute authority of Scripture—have the most followers. There is a tiny but healthy Jewish community as well, and reportedly very little or no anti-Semitism on display or in politics.

In Luxembourg, as in most countries in the West, there has been a dramatic decline in the number of people, especially young adults, who attend a church of any denomination. Despite the residual influence of the Catholic Church, the birth rate is one of the lowest in the world, and the number of divorces has soared. Recruitment of clergy, like church attendance, is also decreasing rapidly. Nevertheless, the Church still fills an important place in the lives of most Luxembourgers.

Despite a decline in church attendance among young people, politics and religion are deeply entwined, and the church dominates many facets of life, including the media and education. The conservative party is intimately linked with the Roman Catholic Church. One influential daily newspaper, the *Luxemburger Wort*, is the official publication of the Christian Social Party and the Catholic Church. Royal family members are all devout Catholics.

Relations between church and state are governed by law. Although there is no one state religion, there are state-recognized religions. Clergy of the officially recognized churches are paid by the state, giving them a civil service status, although they are appointed by their particular religious authority. Religion is a compulsory subject in schools, although a special course on values, morality and social studies was introduced as an alternative some years ago. School holidays are determined by religious holidays.

Notre-Dame Cathedral in the capital city.

PLACES OF WORSHIP

A main center for Luxembourg's Catholics is the Cathedral of Our Lady, known as the Cathédrale Notre-Dame. Built as a Jesuit church between 1613 and 1621, in the Gothic manner, with a Renaissance door, it was enlarged in 1935 with the addition of impressive spires. Noteworthy inside are the massive pillars, with strikingly original ornamentation, and magnificent sculptures and statues.

There is also a crypt containing the burial vaults of various members of the grand ducal family and important bishops. Access to the crypt, which has twelve columns supporting the church above, is by a staircase guarded by two bronze lions bearing the arms of the House of Luxembourg.

Saint Michael's Church stands on the oldest religious site in the city.

Other places of worship in the capital city include the Church of Saint Michael from the tenth century, the Chapel of Saint Quirin (fourteenth century), the Church of Saint John upon the Stone (seventeenth century), and Trinity Church, also known as "the Protestant church" from the nineteenth century.

The countryside is dotted with churches and chapels. The most prominent ones are located in the north, such as in the village of Heiderscheidergrund. The chapel there has a unique octagonal shape called an "inkpot." Built in 1850, it is dedicated to Saint Kunigunda, who is represented in a statue above the door and in a stained-glass window.

Inside the chapel in the town of Esch-sur-Sûre there is an imposing life-size carving of the Gothic Calvary (Christ on the cross and the two thieves). It is one of the most important cultural treasures of the country.

At another village, Bavigne, during World War II, the villagers made a pledge to build a chapel to Our Lady if they survived the Nazi occupation.

Since 1953, the hilltop behind the town has been dominated by three huge oak crosses and the pledged chapel, with a cherished statue of Our Lady on a stone pedestal.

Echternach remains an important religious center. An open-air Mass is celebrated at Echternach each year on Whitsunday to venerate the relics there of Saint Willibrord.

Echternach's Whit Tuesday dancing procession (also called the hopping procession) is Europe's only remaining pageant of this sort.

INTERNET LINKS

http://www.bbc.com/news/magazine-23927021
"Luxembourg's hopping heritage" is an article about the Whit Tuesday dancing procession.

https://www.expedia.com/Notre-Dame-Cathedral-Luxembourg-City. d6077174.Vacation-Attraction
This site offers a slide show of Notre Dame Cathedral in Luxembourg City.

http://www.luxembourg.public.lu/en/le-grand-duche-se-presente/ religion/index.html
This site covers Luxembourg's religious heritage, festivals, communities, and demographics.

LANGUAGE

The name of the National Library in Luxembourg is spelled out in French above the entrance door.

9

WHEN A COUNTRY AS SMALL AS Luxembourg has its own distinct language, its people need to be multilingual, just to get along with the neighbors—which in this case, are never very far away. The national language of Luxembourg is Luxembourgish (LUX-em-borg-gish), or *Lëtzebuergish* (LET-zen-borg-ish). Like Flemish, it is an offshoot of one of the many branches of the Germanic languages. Luxembourgers, however, do not like their tongue to be confused with German.

During the Nazi occupation in 1941, the people voted by an overwhelming 96 percent in a referendum to convey to their oppressors that their language was not German, but Luxembourgish. After the war the public use of Luxembourgish increased dramatically as a natural reaction against four years of suppression. It eventually came to win its full right of use in the grand duchy.

As a country straddling the linguistic frontier, Luxembourg has always represented a meeting place of the cultural and political worlds of both France and Germany. Not surprisingly, French and German are spoken fluently alongside the national language. Each language has a distinct function within the Luxembourgish society.

In an effort to preserve the Luxembourgish language, a petition was circulated in 2016 proposing to make Luxembourgish the country's principal language. Dropping French and German as official languages would "save the Luxembourgish language before it disappears," the petition suggested. Although the petition gathered 14,683 signatures, such a change seems unlikely in the multilingual state.

RIVALRY OF LANGUAGES

While naturally proud of their own language, Luxembourgers realize they are in a unique position—very few outsiders speak it. Therefore French and German are equally important. Still, many consider it common courtesy for people to try to speak the national language of a country that they are in, especially when they are working there.

Consequently, some Luxembourgers may become annoyed when workers from across the border, and even those actually living in the duchy, consistently resist learning and speaking the most basic Luxembourgish words.

Magazines herald the coming royal wedding between Guillaume, the Hereditary Grand Duke of Luxembourg, and the Belgian countess Stephanie de Lannoy.

Luxembourgish was granted the status of an official national language only in 1984. Regardless of that, it has not replaced the use of German or French in written communication. French is generally used for legal and administrative purposes, while German is used in such other areas as religion and newspapers.

For many people, mastering just their own language can be difficult, yet the citizens of Luxembourg learn three in school. In addition, English is also common. Nevertheless, it is important to realize that Luxembourgers, though justifiably proud of their ability to be gracefully trilingual, are native speakers of neither French nor German.

THREE LANGUAGES, THREE USES

The Luxembourgish language is the language used in everyday life within the family and at every level of society. Within the grand duchy, it's spoken by 88.8 percent of the citizens. In the world, however, there are fewer than four hundred thousand people who speak it. Some of these people live in the border regions of Belgium and France. Some US descendants of the late

WHICH OF THESE THINGS IS NOT LIKE THE OTHER?

Compare the names of the months in Luxembourg's three languages. Despite the seemingly great difference of Luxembourgish from the others, the language is actually much more like German than French. Linguistically, in fact, it's a German dialect as well as a language unto itself. Untrained ears hearing people speak Luxembourgish might think they are hearing German.

ENGLISH	GERMAN	FRENCH	LUXEMBOURGISH
January	Januar	janvier	Haartmount
February	Februar	février	Spierkel
March	März	mars	Lenz
April	April	avril	Fréilénk
May	Mai	mai	Päischtmount
June	Juni	juin	Broochmount
July	Juli	juillet	Heemount
August	August	août	Karschnatz
September	September	septembre	Hierschtmount
October	Oktober	octobre	Wäimount
November	November	novembre	Wantermount
December	Dezember	décembre	Krëschtmount

nineteenth-century emigrants may speak it at home.

First and second generation immigrants speak the language of their country of origin. In the workplace, Luxembourgers speak Luxembourgish among themselves, but communicate either in French or German with cross-border workers.

In public life, official notices from the government or the administration are drawn up in French, but the use of Luxembourgish is becoming more widespread. The grand duke and the ministers, for example, now always address the nation in Luxembourgish. Justice in the courtroom is dispensed almost exclusively in French, but witnesses may speak in their mother tongues to avoid misrepresenting themselves. For legal contracts, German and French

A person with a French first name and a Germanic-sounding surname is likely to be from Luxembourg. Because French has been the official written language for so long, most Luxembourgers tend to have French first names or Luxembourgish equivalents. A common name for a boy, Pierre, will also be expressed as Pier (PE-air). Other typical Christian names for boys are Jhang (ZHUNG)—John in English—and Mätt (MAT)—Matthew in English. Popular names for girls are Marrichen (MA-re-hen) or Mari, and Thérèse (TER-es), Theresa. However, this custom of French first names is changing with the rapidly growing immigrant population.

That said, global awareness has certainly entered the registry of new baby names in Luxembourg. Popular baby names in Luxembourg are not much different from international trends in Europe and North America.

In 2015, for example, the most popular girl's name in Luxembourg was Emma, followed closely by Julia, Marie, Lia, and Charlotte. (Charlotte, no doubt, gained popularity from the birth of Princess Charlotte of Cambridge that year to England's Prince William and his wife Kate, the Duchess of Cambridge.) The name Emma was also the most popular girl's name in the United States that year, and Charlotte made it into the top ten as well. And in Germany? Emma came in number 2, and Noah at number 7.

The most popular boy's name in Luxembourg that same year was Matteo, along with Noah, Luca, and Leo. The top boy's name in America that year was Noah. In England, however, Noah limped in that year at number 11.

As in the case with Charlotte, celebrity names influence new parents in Luxembourg as much as anywhere else. However, parents can't get too carried away. Registrars in Luxembourg have the right to refuse names they deem ridiculous, discriminating, against the welfare of the child, or infringing on the rights of third parties.

are the only authorized languages. Advertisements are usually bilingual, but the use of Luxembourgish is increasing significantly. Movie theaters generally screen films in their original language, with French and sometimes German subtitles. The Catholic Church uses German in the majority of its written communications, while sermons are spoken more and more often in Luxembourgish. At school, the language of instruction varies with the level of education. Luxembourgish, introduced only in 1912 as an independent subject, is the language of instruction in preschool education from age four to six, as it is in their homes. Luxembourgish is also the language medium in the first two years of elementary school. While German is introduced as the language of instruction during the first year, French enters the curriculum from the beginning of the second. The three national languages—Luxembourgish, German, and French—thus become the basic language subjects at the elementary level. Luxembourg's secondary education offers, in addition to these three national languages, Latin and English.

LUXEMBOURGISH IN THE ARTS

Although a fair amount of classical and modern literature has been written in Luxembourgish, little of it is well known outside the country. Much of this work is based on themes common in European literature, then adapted to Luxembourgish life.

Humor and satire are key ingredients. Despite so few speakers of the language, literary publishing in Luxembourgish is thriving.

Luxembourgish theater is also very popular. Nearly every village or town puts on at least one theatrical production a year. An occasional feature film and a number of shorts affirm the viability of a small but superior film industry.

STANDARDIZING LUXEMBOURGISH

An official dictionary was introduced to the population in 1950 after several inconclusive attempts to standardize the spelling of written Luxembourgish. Over the years, official government circulars on spelling have been issued, with the last one in 1975. This is a rare example of the success of a legislative measure in imposing regularity upon a previously chaotic linguistic field.

In spite of this, one of the easygoing characteristics of the dialect is the absence of rules and norms, so there is no really uniform language spoken everywhere. An exception to this lack of rules is following the proper way to speak to someone, which is to use the second person singular when the person being addressed is well known or the second person plural when the occasion is more formal or the person is not someone familiar.

When the British Broadcasting Company (BBC) wielded a monopoly over European radio broadcasting in the 1930s, the British public had a very limited choice of programs.

Launched in 1933, the Luxembourg station, Radio Luxembourg, built a huge transmitter to reach British audiences. Programs were based on British-recorded dance music and advertisements, made, ironically, in London and then sent over to be broadcast from Luxembourg. It was the first station to give English listeners what they wanted instead of what was thought they should have. A major diplomatic dispute broke out between the BBC and Radio Luxembourg over this, but the station proved to be a huge success and stayed on the air twenty-four hours a day for almost sixty years, interrupted only by World War II.

Radio Luxembourg was a very international station with German, French, and English services, and even a few weekly broadcasts in Luxembourgish. The English service, broadcast on 208 medium-wave transmissions, came to symbolize nonstop pop music with about two million regular British listeners. The first Beatles record ever heard on radio—"Love Me Do"—was played on Radio Luxembourg in 1962.

One of the more famous Radio Luxembourg disc jockeys was Captain Peter Townsend, who fell in love with a British royal, Princess Margaret, Queen Elizabeth's sister, in 1955. Because he was not a royal himself, and would have had to obtain a divorce in order to marry Margaret, the union was constitutionally barred, which saddened millions of people all over the world. The princess and the captain decided to end their relationship and, sadly, were never to meet again.

When Radio Luxembourg went off the air in 1991, its last words to listeners were the same it had signed off with for half a century—"Goodnight, good listening, and good-bye."

LEARNING LUXEMBOURGISH

For such a small country, there are a staggering number of local and regional variations of its language. Pronunciation varies greatly even within a few miles. In the south the language sounds like a form of brogue, while in the north there is a clear pronunciation of vowels.

Because the dialect is Germanic, many everyday words are German. Because of the influence of French culture, as many as one thousand French words are used in everyday discourse as well. For example, the French word for "station," *gare* (GAR), is used, but it is written as *Gare*, since nouns are spelled with capital letters in Luxembourgish, as in German.

There are many "ch" sounds like the one in *loch*, and "w" is always pronounced as "v." Grammar can vary widely, depending on where one lives. For instance, the plural of the word "man" is *Männer* (MEN-er) in the south and *Män*, as in "men" in English, in the north.

To greet someone, Luxembourgers say *Moien* (MOY-en) or "hello." If inquiring about a person's health, one would say, *Wéi geet et iech* (Vee geet et eech) or "How are you?" Polite phrases, such as *Wann ech glift* (vun ECH glifft) or "please," and *merci* (mare-SEE) or "thanks," are useful words to know.

INTERNET LINKS

http://www.luxembourg.public.lu/en/le-grand-duche-se-presente/langues/utilisation-langues/index.html
This site explains the use of languages in the country.

http://www.omniglot.com/writing/luxembourgish.htm
Omniglot offers a good introduction to Luxembourgish (as well as to French and German), with audio and other links.

http://www.politico.eu/article/migration-mind-your-language-petition-in-luxembourg
This article discusses the debate over expanding the use of Luxembourgish in the Grand Duchy.

ARTS

White globe lights seem to hang in midair in the Mudam modern art gallery in Luxembourg.

10

T HE ARTS AND CULTURE OF Luxembourg is a reflection of its people—diverse and multicultural. The considerable number of immigrants, European Union civil servants living and working in Luxembourg, and the international banking sector, has engendered a flood of national and regional cultural associations from all over Europe, and beyond.

ARCHAEOLOGY

Very few archaeological sites were found in Luxembourg before 1991, when Bastendorf, a Celtic place of worship in the Ardennes, was unearthed. Extensive excavations revealed that the shrine was in use from the first century BCE until the second half of the third century, when it was abandoned during an invasion.

Situated close to water, which was considered a life-giving element with access to the underworld, the shrine disclosed many offerings of silver coins and jewelry, a common method in that age of expressing gratitude or anxiety. Most notable was the discovery of curse boards, small lead tablets folded in such a way that the five-line curse would not be visible. Placed in the stream bed of the shrine, these curses would then be fulfilled by the gods of the underworld—it was hoped. It is thought

In 2004, to mark the 125th anniversary of the birth of Luxembourg-born, world-renowned photographer Edward Steichen, the grand duchy created the Edward Steichen Award Luxembourg. This contemporary art prize is awarded every two years to a young European artist. He or she wins the opportunity to work and train in New York City—thereby recognizing Steichen's links to both New York and Luxembourg.

A professional restores an ancient Roman mural of a leaping ibex discovered at a site in the rural village of Vichten.

that there were regular gatherings at Bastendorf for religious festivals that included the sacrifice of animals.

Another important archaeological discovery was made in 1995 when a farmer from the town of Vichten, in the north, discovered by chance a 72-square yard (60-square m) Roman mosaic on his land. The floor mosaic represents the nine muses who, in Greek mythology, are the daughters of the great god Zeus and Mnemosyne, a Titan representing memory. The muses were thought to inspire music, the arts, and the sciences. The stunning find, dating from 240 CE, has proved to be one of the largest and best preserved mosaic works of its kind north of the Alps.

Other archaeological sites in Luxembourg include the Roman baths near the town of Mamer and at four other sites north of the capital city. A Celtic tomb dating from the first century BCE was found in Clemency. Another site of interest is the Gallo-Roman complex at Echternach, on the Sûre River, developed between 50 and 400 CE. The lower sections of a seventy-room villa have been reconstructed, although some of the original stonework is still visible. The extensive Roman remains lie alongside medieval ramparts and an eighth-century abbey founded by the first Anglo-Saxon missionary working on the continent, Saint Willibrord.

One of the twentieth century's foremost photographers was Edward Steichen (1879–1973). Born in Bivange, Luxembourg, he came to the United States as an infant with his parents,  and grew up as an American. As a young artist, he worked with photographer Alfred Stieglitz to promote photography as a fine art. The two founded a gallery in New York City for the promotion of avante-garde European artists, such as Henri Matisse, Paul Cézanne, and Pablo Picasso, as well as to introduce American audiences to art photography. In 1904, Steichen began experimenting with color photography and produced some important work in the early days of that genre.

In his later years, Steichen served as the director of photography at the Museum of Modern Art (MOMA) in New York. During that time, he curated the renowned exhibit, The Family of Man, which opened at MOMA in 1955. The show, a collection of 503 photographs by 273 photographers from 68 countries, was thematically centered on peace and brotherhood, the universality of the human experience, and the common ties between cultures and countries. It was a response to the geopolitical tensions of the Cold War era, the arms race, and fears of the atomic bomb. The exhibit toured the world for eight years, and was published as a book, which has never been out of print. Steichen called the exhibit "the culmination of my career."

Today, the original collection, now restored, is archived and displayed at Clervaux Castle in Luxembourg, according to Steichen's wishes. In 2003, UNESCO added The Family of Man to its Memory of the World Register in recognition of its historical value. The Memory of the World Register is a compendium of documents, manuscripts, oral traditions, audio-visual materials, library, and archival holdings that UNESCO has deemed to be of universal value.

THEATER AND CINEMA

The recently renovated Grand Theater of the City of Luxembourg, built in 1964, is the largest venue in the country. During the annual theater season, an international festival of operas, plays, concerts, and ballets with multicultural themes is held. Luxembourg is also a regular stop for many touring theater companies producing various types of plays, including social commentaries.

The town of Wiltz in the Ardennes is the setting for the open-air International Theater Festival in its castle's amphitheater. Each year in July, world-famous actors perform there for audiences from all over Europe.

The Centre National de l'Audiovisuel (CNA), or National Audiovisual Center, created in 1989, is an institution for the preservation, restoration, and production of Luxembourg's films and photography. The Centre provides a history of filmmaking in Luxembourg—the first movie ever made there was shot in 1899, four years after the historic Lumière in Paris projected the world's first public films. An annual film festival shows many new short films that are directed by budding Luxembourg talents.

MUSIC

Classical music is very popular with Luxembourgers, who support the Luxembourg Philharmonic (OPL), the Luxembourg Chamber Orchestra (OCL), and several other musical ensembles. The Grande-Duchesse Joséphine-Charlotte Concert Hall, also known as the Philharmonie Luxembourg, opened in 2005 in the capital city. Now the home of the OCL, the architecturally impressive venue hosts some four hundred performances a year of not only classical music, but jazz, world music, pop, and other forms. Concerts are also popular throughout the year at the Conservatory of Music in the city suburbs.

The European Soloists Luxembourg, founded in 1989, is an ensemble that unites the best musicians from famous European orchestras in a first-class chamber orchestra, under the direction of German conductor Christoph König. It particularly looks to promote young talent. The orchestra has found a home in the north of Luxembourg, where rehearsals are held. Supported by many patrons, including members of the grand ducal family, it has given many

The Philharmonic concert hall is the capital city's major music venue.

concerts in Luxembourg and in such other European cities as Frankfurt, Budapest, and Paris.

Popular music of all kinds—from jazz to hip hop to electronica—has many fans, as well as artists and bands. Each June, the grand duchy hosts the Fête de la Musique, an outdoor summertime music festival that takes place across the country that celebrates all styles of music, and features top international musicians. The town of Roeser, in the southern part of the country, is the site of the annual open-air Rock-a-Field festival, a rock celebration that lasts for three days. In July, the capital city sponsors the annual World MeYouZik Festival, featuring world music and other multicultural events. This celebration finds a ready audience in the city, where 67 percent of the people are not native Luxembourgers.

PAINTING AND SCULPTURE

Roses painted by the renowned Pierre-Joseph Redouté.

Luxembourg City boasts four major art museums— the Luxembourg Casino Forum for Contemporary Art; the Luxembourg Museum of Modern Art (MUDAM); Villa Vauban, the art museum of City of Luxembourg, housing primarily Dutch and French paintings of the seventeenth through nineteenth centuries; and the National Museum of History and Art (MNHA).

Unlike many other European countries, the reputation of Luxembourg's artists is not an international one. While there are no great masters from a past age whose achievements can be extolled or whose paintings hang on gallery walls, Luxembourg has produced a number of artists who deserve recognition.

Born in Saint Hubert in the Ardennes, Pierre-Joseph Redouté(1759—1840) began, at the age of thirteen, a career that was to make him the most influential botanical artist of all time. In Paris he worked for Emperor Napoleon's wife, Josephine, creating over six hundred vellum drawings that are studied to this day.

NICO KLOPP

Nico Klopp ((1894–1930), the son of a wine grower along the Moselle River, studied at the Royal Prussian Academy of Art in Dusseldorf. There he met his future wife and produced his first expressionist woodcuts. Eventually, separated from his wife and daughter, he returned to Luxembourg and survived by selling paintings, preparing illustrations for periodicals, and raising rabbits. Despite living in a small town in the Moselle Valley, where artists were not greatly admired, he never gave up painting and engraving. Forced by financial circumstances, he ultimately became a local tax collector.

Le port de Martigues (1929)

The first of Klopp's paintings were characterized by tragic romanticism. Later works were even more severe, but with a splendid power of light. Often his work met with harsh criticism at home. It prompted debates between art critics who defended classical academic art and others who espoused the avant-garde school of expressionism. Klopp himself never took up the battle in the name of his art, although he was a driving force behind the organization of the first "secessionist" exhibition in Luxembourg in 1927. Significantly, that was sixty-three years after exhibitions in Paris of Manet and others.

The sole demand of life that Klopp made was recognition of his artistic work. For him beauty was the only purpose of art, and he broke away from academic prerequisites and rules, which at that time were the only criteria for the appraisal of art. Sadly, his pursuit of beauty was never understood. Although it meant forgoing financial security, he remained true to his ideal of beauty and of its expression in art. While he achieved a degree of recognition abroad, he was never able to convert this into financial success.

Klopp's early death from meningitis, in 1930, at age thirty-six, marked the end of the secessionist period in Luxembourg. The work of Nico Klopp achieved a belated breakthrough only after World War II, with three retrospective exhibitions finally bringing posthumous understanding, appreciation, and respect.

Joseph Kutter 's famous painting, *Head of a Clown* (1937)

Joseph Kutter (1894—1941) was an expressionist painter who introduced modern art to Luxembourg, and is considered one of Luxembourg's most important painters. He painted landscapes and portraits, but some of his most famous paintings, late in his life, portrayed haunting clowns who seemed to be battling inner torment.

The eighteenth century master sculptors Nicholas Jacques and Jean Georges Scholtus are well known in Luxembourg for their beautiful baroque high altars found in many of the old churches in the Ardennes and Mullerthal areas of the country. The War Memorial, a modern sculpture, is the work of Claus Cito, the victor in an international sculpture competition in 1923.

CULTURAL MONUMENTS AND ARCHITECTURE

In 1994 the World Heritage Committee of UNESCO placed the old town and fortifications of Luxembourg City on its list of world cultural monuments. Divided into three areas, the first site takes in the ancient quarters, including the original rock the city was founded on. The second area encompasses the governmental quarter, the palace, and the cathedrals. The third contains the battlements and towers that secured the city to the east from the fourteenth century onward.

Over the centuries, Luxembourg has seen many architectural changes. Many farmhouses from the sixteenth and seventeenth centuries still exist, recognizable by their Renaissance-style front doors with coats of arms and partly mullioned windows. The bigger farms often had a large entrance gate to the courtyard. During the eighteenth century, equally impressive farmhouses were built. Typically, these had symmetrical white facades, window lintels in the shape of segmental arches, and beautifully sculptured oaken front doors framed with stone.

By the nineteenth century, the most significant buildings being constructed were the manor houses, which retained the symmetrical fronts and stone frames of earlier eras.

INTERNET LINKS

http://www.luxembourg.public.lu/en/le-grand-duche-se-presente/culture/index.html
This site presents a wide range of arts information and links.

https://www.theguardian.com/artanddesign/gallery/2015/nov/06/the-family-of-man-photography-united-the-planet-edward-steichen
A gallery of images from *The Family of Man* exhibit are presented on this site.

http://www.unesco.org/new/en/communication-and-information/memory-of-the-world/register/full-list-of-registered-heritage/registered-heritage-page-3/family-of-man
The UNESCO listing for *The Family of Man* is found on this site.

http://whc.unesco.org/en/list/699
The UNESCO World Heritage listing for the City of Luxembourg is presented on this page.

LEISURE

People enjoy a summer afternoon at an outdoor café near Place de Clairefontaine in Luxembourg City.

11

LUXEMBOURGERS ENJOY A BETTER work-life balance than people in most other countries, which means they have plenty of time for leisure activities. Although the legal work week is limited to forty hours (except for certain situations), the average work week is about twenty-nine hours. In addition, Luxembourgers have at least thirty-two days of vacation a year. Nevertheless, Luxembourgers have earned a reputation for working hard and taking life seriously.

VACATIONS

For many Luxembourgers, vacations are more often spent abroad than at home. With no beaches or mountain resorts in Luxembourg, there is little opportunity for the swimming, sunbathing, or skiing that other parts of Europe offer.

Moreover, Luxembourg's climate does not really attract Luxembourgers to spend their time off in their own country. Warmth and sunshine in the Mediterranean beckon those who can afford it. Reasonably priced package holidays are easily available.

Employment on Sunday is prohibited in Luxembourg, except in certain instances, such as emergency response, security, and industries that rely on continuous processes (steel, glass, and chemical industries). Working on a Sunday entitles the employee to a pay increase of 70 percent. Alternatively, employees may be compensated for each hour worked on a Sunday with additional free time.

Aurelien Joachim (22), celebrates his team's first goal during the FIFA 2018 World Cup Qualifier between Luxembourg and France at the Stade Josy Bartel on March 25, 2017.

NATIONAL SPORTS

Luxembourgers enjoy sports activities, both to play and the watch. There are many sports associations in the country, covering all disciplines. Luxembourg's true national sport is soccer (called football in Europe), which is played at the international level at the European championship matches. American football has never really caught the imagination of Luxembourgers in the same way as soccer. The national soccer team is nicknamed the Red Lions, in reference to the emblem on the country's coat of arms. The team plays its home games at the Stade Josy Barthel in Luxembourg City, which is named for Luxembourg's only Olympic gold medalist (at the 1952 Summer Games), Josy Barthel. The stadium, which accommodates eight thousand

Luxembourg participates in the Olympics, but competing against nations with much greater populations makes for a great disadvantage. To "level the playing field," so to speak, the National Olympic Committees of eight small European countries created the Games of the Small States of Europe (GSSE). From its initial forming at the 1984 Olympics until 2009, there were eight members; the group's ninth member, Montenegro, was added in 2009. Today they include Andorra, Cyprus, Iceland, Lichtenstein, Luxembourg, Malta, Monaco, Montenegro, and San Marino. Members all have a population of less than one million people (Cyprus is the only exception; however its population was below one million in 1984).

The home team enters the sixth Small European States Games in Luxembourg.

The games take place in the late spring, at the end of May or beginning of June, and the participating countries rotate hosting duties. Luxembourg hosted the GSSE in 2013. That year featured eleven kinds of Olympic sports in both men's and women's divisions—athletics, basketball, beach volleyball, cycling, gymnastic, judo, shooting, swimming, table tennis, tennis, and volleyball.

With much improved odds, the athletes from these tiny nations can strive for medals—and win them. So far, Iceland leads the pack in medals, with Luxembourg coming in third with a total of 988!

spectators, dates from 1931 and doesn't meet the necessary standards to host the qualifying matches for the European soccer championships. A new national stadium, "Lentille," seating 9,595, is planned in Kockelscheuer, with construction to begin in 2017, and the expected opening in 2019. It will also host rugby games.

Basketball, with national leagues for women as well as men, is an increasingly popular game and participation in the European championships is taken seriously. Tennis is another popular sport, with more than fifty tennis clubs in the small country. An indoor tennis tournament, the Luxembourg Open, takes place every year. Equestrian events, like show jumping and dressage, are also held annually at Cup level.

Many people enjoy cycling, which is suited to the country's largely flat terrain. The Tour de Luxembourg is an annual bicycle race that begins and ends in Luxembourg City, covering 428 miles (689 km) in four stages over four days. Typically held the first week of June, it attracts cyclists from throughout Europe and the United States and is something of a preview to the better-known Tour de France.

RECREATION

With a dense network of marked walking paths and special pedestrian circuits through the forests in the Ardennes, hiking is a popular activity among Luxembourgers. Totally leaving civilization behind is difficult to achieve, though, as one is never more than five miles (8 km) away from a village or farm.

For those who wish to extend hiking excursions into more than day trips, campgrounds are everywhere, and numerous youth hostels are well situated close to campsites should the weather turn rainy. Even in the southern industrial part of the country, walking trails, some up to 73 miles (117 km) long, can be found.

Bicycling is a national pastime. It is not uncommon to see elderly people cycling, too. In the summer the weather is especially inviting for biking through the not-too-difficult Luxembourg terrain. There are traffic-free bicycle trails over much of Luxembourg along the scenic main rivers.

Kayaking and canoeing, as well as other water-related pastimes, are becoming increasingly pursued because of the country's many rivers. Luxembourg also has a number of golf courses. Rock climbing, fishing, and hunting are all popular activities. Horseback riding is a particular favorite.

ENTERTAINMENT

Nightlife is excellent in Luxembourg, as there is a good mix of bars, restaurants, and clubs run by Luxembourgers as well as other nationalities—one can play darts in British pubs or sing in Japanese karaoke bars. In these well-patronized nightspots, mainstream live music from piano to folk to blues and rock can be found.

International music groups of all sorts perform regularly in the grand duchy. The capital is ideally situated to attract crowds of young people from neighboring parts of Germany, France, and Belgium because it is within such easy reach.

Other ways Luxembourgers spend their time include watching television, going to movies, and visiting cafés, the equivalent of bars. American and other movies are released early in Luxembourg and are dubbed in French and German.

A bike rests against a marker on the Troisvierges portion of the Vennbahn, a bicycle path that passes through Germany, Belgium, and Luxembourg.

INTERNET LINKS

http://www.luxembourg.public.lu/en/vivre/sports/index.html
A calendar of annual sports events is included on this site.

http://www.visitluxembourg.com/en/what-to-do/sport-leisure
This tourist site covers many of the leisure activities available in the duchy.

FESTIVALS

Grapes ripen in the vineyards of the Mosell Valley on the Luxembourg–Germany border.

12

LUXEMBOURG'S HOLIDAY TRADITIONS incorporate European cultural motifs, Roman Catholic church customs, ancient pagan rites, and some festivities that are distinctively Luxembourgish. For such a tiny country, it certainly has plenty of its own idiosyncratic traditions, which only add to the fun.

In the Moselle wine-producing region, people enjoy festivals of both wine and grapes. In the springtime, villages hold wine festivals outdoors featuring live music and traditional foods. Grape festivals are usually held in October, as a thanksgiving for a good grape harvest. In some villages, a "grape queen" parades though town handing out wine. In Schwebsange, the town fountain flows with wine!

The Schueberfouer, a fair dating from 1340, is the grand duchy's largest annual fair and now features an amusement park.

CUSTOMS AND RITUALS

Dräikinneksdag, celebrated on January 6, is Christian Feast of the Epiphany, marking the day when the three kings, or Magi, came to visit the baby Jesus. On this day a special almond cake called *galette des rois* ("kings' cake") is baked, containing a miniature figure of a king. In the days of old, the cake contained a simple, plain bean.

The fortunate person whose piece of cake yields the king's figure—usually one of the children, of course—is appointed king for the day or even a whole week, and dons a golden cardboard crown This lucky youngster enjoys certain privileges, such as the right to decide on the family's meals for the next few days.

Bretzelsonndeg (BRET-zel-son-deg) in March or April is Pretzel Sunday. The date changes as it marks the third Sunday of Lent. Although the sequence of events is the subject of some debate, according to tradition, a young man offers his girlfriend a sweet present on Valentine's Day to proclaim his love. If she responds favorably by offering him a pretzel on Pretzel Sunday, he then confirms his intentions by presenting her with decorated eggs at Easter. Thus Pretzel Sunday has become a day dedicated to lovers and is celebrated by displays of folk art.

Schueberfouer (SHOO-bare-foor) is celebrated on September 3. Originally a shepherds' market, founded in 1340 by Count John the Blind, it has become the capital's annual giant funfair. It opens when sheep decorated with colorful ribbons are led by shepherds, dressed in folk costume, through the inner quarters of the city. They are accompanied by a band playing a lively tune—the "Hammelsmarsch" (HAMM-els-marsh), the sheep's march. Everyone enjoys the fair's eateries, Ferris wheel, bumper cars, and the friendly bustle.

NEW YEAR'S

New Year's Eve, marking the end of the year, is celebrated more with friends, rather than just family. This can be either at home or in a restaurant. Many of those who eat at home, watching television, will venture out to one of the many "Sylvester" balls, so named because December 31 is Saint Sylvester's

NATIONAL HOLIDAYS IN LUXEMBOURG

January 1	New Year's Day
March/April	Easter, Easter Monday
May 1	Labor Day/May Day
May/June	Ascension Day
May/June	Whitsun (Pentecost), Whit Monday
June 23	National Day
August 15	Assumption of Mary
November 1	All Saints' Day
December 25	Christmas Day
December 26	Saint Stephen's Day (Boxing Day)

Day. These are happy dances in honor of the year ahead. At midnight everyone wishes each other a happy New Year, and people kiss, pop champagne corks, and light fireworks outdoors. The capital city, in particular, gets caught up in the party mood. The atmosphere is one of carnival-style decorations and firecrackers, which add up to a noisy and colorful celebration.

New Year's Day, a public holiday devoted to sleeping late and visiting the family, may seem dull to many Luxembourgers compared with the previous night's excitement, but it is well enjoyed. The prime minister traditionally makes a New Year's speech on television as a kickoff to the year.

EASTER

In this predominantly Catholic country, Easter is a very important holiday which marks the crucifixion and subsequent resurrection of Christ. Many people attend Mass on the holy days leading up to Easter Sunday, as well as on the joyous day itself. It's a day for family and feasting. In addition to its religious observances, the festival is replete with many customs, some of which harken back to pre-Christian times—signifying fertility, springtime, rebirth, and renewal.

On Good Friday, three days before Easter Sunday, a tradition called *Klibberegoen* (KLI-bare-gurn), or "Rattles Round," takes place. According to legend, all the bells in the parish churches fall silent at this time and fly away to Rome for the pope's blessing. To replace the church bells, local boys and girls walk through the village streets singing and shaking *klibbers*, rattles that have a characteristic dry sound.

After the return of the bells to the churches, the youngsters call on each house to collect brightly colored Easter eggs. Other children walk in a procession behind a dog-rose bush, covered in paper flowers and multicolored ribbons, called the *Jaudes* (YOW-des) or "Judas," for the apostle who betrayed Jesus Christ. After the last Rattles Round has taken place, the Jaudes is burned.

Peckvillercher bird whistles are a traditional feature of the Emaischen festival on Easter Monday.

On Easter Sunday children traditionally hunt for Easter eggs hidden by the *Ouschterhues* or "Easter Bunny." Once the eggs have all been found, the children play *Técken*, or "the battle of the eggs," a friendly competition in which kids knock their eggs against each other's eggs. Those whose shells break are the losers. Typically, the four-day Easter holiday is celebrated with the first real spring outing of the year. By this time, the weather will have improved and there is a two-week school vacation.

Easter Monday is a public holiday. In the capital's old town a traditional colorful market called *Émaischen* (Eh-MAY-schen), or "Feast of Emmaus," takes place. Once, only utilitarian pottery and other household wares were displayed, but now popular arts and crafts are the main items, including the small whistling pottery birds called *peckvillercher*. There are also games for children, folk dances, and singing.

NATIONAL DAY

A color guard marches on National Day in Luxembourg City.

Luxembourgers celebrate the birthday of their grand duke on June 23, although his actual birthday is in April. This holiday is also considered the country's National Day. Many Luxembourgers use this day for shopping trips across the border, where it is not a public holiday. All over the country, National Day is an occasion for a happy and festive celebration, with traditional and patriotic processions, religious services, concerts, and public dances.

Festivities start on the day before with members of the grand ducal family being welcomed in various towns and villages of the country. In the evening, Luxembourg City is flooded with lights and a torchlight parade is held, followed by a large fireworks display. On the day itself, crowds gather to watch a military parade. This is followed by a religious service in the cathedral, in the presence of the grand ducal family.

Afterward all the ducal family members make a public appearance on the balcony of the palace. On successive evenings for the rest of the week, various receptions of the diplomatic corps and national notables are held in the palace.

Luxembourg has a long history of fetes and fairs, which are always accompanied by colorful processions, musical bands, flowers, and parades. Every village has its own *Kiermes* (KEER-mes), or village fair, on the anniversary of the birthday of its local saint.

Carnival week is a time of carefree fun before the somber Catholic season of Lent calendar begins, which marks the forty days before Easter. and coincides with a one-week school holiday. During this time, the "Carnival Prince" reigns supreme.

In the afternoons there are processions with floats, sessions of public readings, and theme pageants. Costume balls are held in the evenings, with the musicians also in disguise. On Ash Wednesday, which is the beginning of Lent, young people in the Moselle valley carry a huge straw doll through the streets. On a bridge over the Moselle, they set fire to the doll and throw it into the river to herald the end of the joyful carnival.

February 2 is *Liichtemëss* (LICH-ter-mess). This is an end-of-winter ritual devoted to the "new light," or the end of the short, dark days of winter. Children go from house to house carrying candles and lamps and singing traditional songs. Their rewards nowadays are candies, but in olden times, they received more basic necessities, such as lard and peas.

On February 25, *Buurgbrennen* (BORG-bren-en),or Bonfire Day, takes place. This is another end-of-winter custom from pagan days. Groups of people from various associations such as Boy Scouts, Girl Guides (Girl Scouts), music societies, and fire brigades gather on nearby hills and set fire to giant crosses made of wood and straw. The idea is to expel the darkness of winter. This pagan ritual of burning crosses (which shows the influence of Christianity) forms a chain all over the hills, and is accompanied with barbecues and hot red wine.

The first week in May is the beginning of spring fetes, when members of local societies enter the woods to cut the first green branches. These are fashioned into 4-foot (1.2-m) diameter crowns, symbols of the reawakening of nature, called *Meekranz* (MEE-krantz), which are then carried in processions, led by bands in most villages.

OTHER RELIGIOUS FESTIVALS

Luxembourgers have no shortage of special days to brighten the calendar. Religious festivals add spiritual meaning to the seasons.

OCTAVE The two-week religious festival of *Octave* (or *Oktav*), starting on the third Sunday after Easter, is focused on a pilgrimage in honor of Our Lady of Luxembourg, to the Cathédrale Notre-Dame in Luxembourg City. Delegations from parishes in all the counties participate in this pilgrimage. Many have to leave home in the night to get there on time, usually traveling on foot as part of the pilgrimage. On the square in front of the cathedral, a fairground atmosphere prevails, with stands selling fried fish, candy, and religious souvenirs. The end of Octave on the fifth Sunday after Easter is marked with a closing ceremony, when stately, solemn processions are held with the royal family and various Catholic dignitaries from abroad taking part in this grand occasion.

Since 1666, Catholics of the grand duchy and neighboring regions have come to the festival to venerate Our Lady, the "Comforter of the Afflicted." The cult of Our Lady remains important to Luxembourg, even in an increasingly lay society, as it also symbolizes national identity and independence. On Ascension Day, another pilgrimage to a nearby shrine dedicated to Our Lady of Fatima takes place.

WHITSUN is the name given to the religious time of Pentecost, and it usually falls on the last weekend of May or early June. In the town of Kaundorf, a procession across fields and forests to Saint Pirmin's fountain is held. According to legend, Saint Pirmin was cured of an eye disease at the beginning of the eighth century after rinsing his eyes in the waters of the spring. Healing virtues are still attached to these waters.

Whit Tuesday, although not an official holiday, marks the "dancing procession" in Echternach, Luxembourg's oldest city. It's held in honor of Saint Willibrord, the patron saint of Luxembourg, who died in Echternach in 739. This unique religious tradition, also called the "hopping procession of Echternach," was intended, in medieval times, as a protection against epilepsy. Recognized since 2010 as a UNESCO Intangible Cultural Heritage, it attracts thousands of pilgrims and spectators each year.

Some eight thousand dancers, in rows eight or nine wide, traditionally take three steps forward and two steps back. They are joined to each other by white handkerchiefs. Fiddlers and other musicians play haunting polkas to accompany each group of dancers. This colorful procession, which also includes a large number of priests, nuns, and monks, winds its way through the old cobbled streets of Echternach before returning to the Basilica church.

ASSUMPTION DAY *Léiffrawëschdag* (LEEF-frow-wusch-dag), in August, is cause for another large celebration in honor of the Virgin Mary. Various herbs, corn, and other plants are gathered into bouquets, which are presented as offerings at various country chapels.

ALL SAINTS' DAY November 1 is a day for religious ceremonies in churchyards. The tombs are blessed, and memories of the dead are revered by family members meeting at the graves of their relatives. The ceremonies are usually followed by gatherings at home or in a restaurant.

Men perform the traditional Whit Monday hopping dance in honor of St. Willibrord in Echternach.

CHRISTMAS

A two-week school vacation occurs around Christmas, and many families go abroad to escape the cold weather. Stores everywhere during this season are aglitter with decorations, while in the streets everything is festooned and illuminated for the season of happiness and goodwill.

Christmas festivities begin on the feast of *Niklosdag* (NICK-los-dag), Saint Nicholas Day, on December 6. Each year *Kleeschen* (CLE-schen), or Father Christmas, dressed in a bishop's vestments and holding a staff, comes down from the skies to reward the children who have been good throughout the year.

He is accompanied, in the European tradition, not by elves or reindeer, but by a dark companion who frightens naughty children. The Luxembourgish version of this fellow is named *Housecker* (HUSE-eck-er).

Dressed in a hooded monk's robe, he carries long sticks or switches with which he chastises badly-behaved children. Saint Nick and his sidekick are welcomed in the various towns and villages. After a procession, Saint Nicholas gives sweets to the children who, until about the age of eight, also get some presents on this day.

Lights attract shoppers at the Christmas Market in Luxembourg City.

THE AMERICAN SAINT NICK

The Christmas of 1944, during World War II, was a terrible time in the tiny town of Wiltz in northwest Luxembourg. Four years of German occupation had taken a dreadful toll, and the region had only just been liberated the previous September. That autumn, a company of US soldiers fresh from battle—the 112th Regiment of the 28th Infantry Division, Pennsylvania National Guard—had been sent to Wiltz for rest and recuperation.

As Christmas approached, some of the Americans decided to throw a holiday party on December 6 for the war-weary Luxembourgers. In Europe, December 6 is Saint Nicholas Day, a festive occasion featuring Old Saint Nick himself. However, the people of Wiltz hadn't celebrated anything—not even Christmas—in nearly five years of war. They had gone a long time in fear and deprivation.

For the party, US army cooks baked treats and the GIs somehow rounded up enough candy and other goodies from their own care packages sent from home. Twenty-two-year-old Corporal Richard Brookins, from Rochester, New York, agreed to play Saint Nicholas.

He borrowed a mitre hat and long flowing robes from the local priest, and did his best to concoct a long beard. On the day of the festivities, the American "Saint Nick" rode through town on the back of an open Army Jeep, flanked by two little girls dressed as angels. He handed out little treats to the village children as other soldiers sang and played music. The party continued at Wiltz Castle with much merriment. Shortly afterward, the Americans had to leave the town and move on to the next battle on the march to Berlin.

Ten days later after the party, on December 16, the German Army launched a surprise offensive in the region. What came to be called the Battle of the Bulge destroyed Wiltz and killed many of the villagers, including children. US forces suffered some one hundred thousand casualties during the more-than-a-month-long battle.

Brookins survived the war. Thirty years later, the village of Wiltz invited him to return to play the American Saint Nick once again. The people had never forgotten him and honored him every Christmas season. He returned several times, even at age ninety-two, to play Santa to a new generation of children, who, thankfully, live in peace.

Christmas Eve is family time when children, parents, and grandparents gather around their Christmas tree, listen to carols, and enjoy a sumptuous meal, often of ham or roast pork. Christmas Eve is also one of the few times in the year when children are allowed to stay up later than usual. Frequently, the whole family attends Midnight Mass celebrating the birth of Jesus Christ. Many workers are granted unofficial leave from their jobs for the afternoon.

On Christmas Day, a lunch, interrupted only by a televised speech to the nation by the grand duke, is usually hosted by an older member of the family, such as a grandparent. People may be feeling somewhat lethargic after all the eating of the preceding evening. Saint Stephen's Day, *Stiefesdag* (SHTEEF-fes-dag), the day after Christmas, is another holiday, with yet more feasting.

INTERNET LINKS

http://www.cnn.com/2009/WORLD/europe/12/22/luxembourg.santa
This article tells the story of Dick Brookins, "the American Santa," and his return to Luxembourg in 2009.

http://www.luxembourg.public.lu/en/le-grand-duche-se-presente/fetes-traditions/index.html
This Luxembourg site highlights the duchy's many festivals and traditions.

https://www.timeanddate.com/holidays/luxembourg
This site lists the current calendar of holidays in Luxembourg.

http://www.unesco.org/culture/ich/en/RL/hopping-procession-of-echternach-00392
The UNESCO site describes the significance of the dancing procession.

FOOD

Blue grapes from the Provence region of France are displayed in a basket at a market in Luxembourg.

13

LUXEMBOURG'S CULINARY TRADITION is rich, hearty, country-style food, heavily influenced by German cuisine. It tends to be plain but flavorful meat and potatoes or pork and beans fare—the sort that rural people put on their dinner tables for many generations. *Huesenziwwi,* or jugged hare, is just such a dish, which is, or at least was, popular during hunting season. Some younger Luxembourgers claim only old people eat these sorts of traditional foods today.

Although German is the primary fare, French influence is seen in elegant dishes such as *Bouchée à la Reine*, chicken and mushrooms in a creamy white wine sauce served in a puff pastry shell. Generally, Luxembourgers like to combine French quality with German quantity. Large portions are standard in restaurants and homes.

Naturally, in today's world, Luxembourgers also enjoy a wide range of international foods. Italian and Portuguese immigrants brought their cuisines with them to the Duchy, and the usual fast food fare, such as burgers and fries, is available in the city.

Two dishes that are frequently called Luxembourg's "national dishes" are *Judd mat Gaardebounen,* a smoked pork neck braised with broad beans and potatoes, and *Bounenschlupp,* a green bean and potato soup cooked with bacon. Both dishes contain the word *bounen,* which is Luxembourgish for "bean."

TRADITIONAL FARE

There are a number of dishes that are considered traditional rural cooking. Such meals are simple and homely in style, but nourishing and wholesome in content.

Typically a first course would be *Bounenschlupp* (BORN-nen-shlup), a bean soup. Many types of beans can be used, but the most common is the green bean. Also eaten as an appetizer are *Quenelles* (keh-nells), small oval-shaped dumplings, stuffed with ground meat or fish. Fish *Quenelles* are prepared with a rich cream sauce, while the meat versions have an equally rich brown sauce.

Quenelles are ready to be simmered in a fish or meat stock.

After the soup or appetizer, a main course follows. Sometimes *Quenelles*, usually meat ones, are eaten as a main meal. Such a dish would be accompanied by sauerkraut and boiled potatoes. One very popular dish is *Judd mat Gaardebounen* (Yudd mat gard-DA-born-nen), smoked neck of pork in a delicious herb sauce, accompanied by broad beans (often called fava beans in the United States) and boiled potatoes. Another is *Träipen* (TRY-pen), a type of black pudding, or sausage, usually served with horseradish, mashed potatoes, and sauerkraut.

Feierstengszalot (fire-STENG-za-lot), a salad composed of sliced cold beef with hard-cooked egg and onions in an oil and vinegar dressing, is a quick and tasty meal. A more acquired taste is *Kuddelfleck* (KU-del-fleck), boiled tripe, which comes from the stomach lining of cattle and is classified as offal. Resembling a honeycomb in appearance, tripe is rich in gelatin, calcium, and iron, with very low caloric value. Tripe usually requires prolonged cooking, but it is often sold partly cooked and blanched. *Gras Double Provençal* (grah doobl proh-vahn-SAL), tripe cooked with onion, garlic, and white wine, is a thrifty and flavorful dish.

Delicious Ardennes ham, or *Fierkelsjhelli* (fear-KUL-hel-la), roasted suckling pig covered in an aspic sauce, is reserved for more special occasions. It is usually followed by cheese, particularly *Kachkéis* (KARCH-kays), a typical soft and sticky boiled cheese. Dessert is not normally served with everyday meals, but can be expected to make an appearance at weekend tables, as would liqueurs.

Ardennes ham is thin-sliced for serving.

EATING HABITS

Luxembourgers enjoy a large variety of vegetables, either grown locally or imported from Belgium and the Netherlands. A wide variety of exotic fruit from Asia and South America can also be found in the markets. Meat, fish, and game are popular, prepared either in a traditional manner or in a slightly more sophisticated style inspired by French cuisine.

Most working Luxembourgers eat little, if any, breakfast, unless they are on vacation and have that extra time. Coffee, rarely tea, bread, and jam is standard—a Continental breakfast. Lunch was once the most important meal, but because of modern working habits and short lunch breaks, the main meal is now taken in the evening, typically between 6:30 and 7:30. One main course is served, with soup as a starter. Cheese is reserved for formal occasions or Sunday meals.

Many workers in the service industries in the capital take their lunch in restaurants, all of which offer varying menus of the day. Great efforts are being made to install cafeterias in schools, which at present close between 12 and 2, when students go home for lunch.

A traditional family outing is Sunday lunch or, increasingly, brunch. The meal usually takes the form of a buffet that includes hot dishes. Meals accompanying special occasions, such as anniversaries, success at exams, baptism, first communion, and confirmation, which used to be eaten at home, are now more frequently hosted in restaurants.

Handmade treats are displayed in a candy store.

SPECIALTIES

Pastries and assorted chocolates are a special feature in the Luxembourg pastry shops. A true specialty is *Quetschentaart* (ketch-en-TART), an irresistible tart made from small plums and the plum liqueur Quetsch.

The best chocolates are those made by hand, using the finest chocolate, fresh cream, and butter, with no added preservatives. Some contain fruit and nuts, while others use liqueur. Somewhat expensive, they are intended for the true connoisseur. Freshly made the day before they are sold, they will not last more than three days, but the difference in taste between these and factory-made ones makes this disadvantage worthwhile.

During carnival season, or Lent, a special pastry called *Les Pensées Brouillées* (lay PON-say BREW-il-lay), literally "puzzled thoughts," is available in abundance. These are delicious fried knots of dough and are a favorite with young and old alike.

WINES

A vineyard in Remich in the Moselle Valley.

Wines from the Moselle Valley have gained a reputation as quality wines for everyday consumption. They are completely different in taste, though not in names, from their German Moselle counterparts. Luxembourg wines are less sweet and resemble those from France.

Luxembourg's Moselle region enjoys a very developed wine-growing culture. With temperatures slightly above the national average and rainfall spread throughout the year, the region provides the ideal climate for producing great wines.

The Moselle Valley, which flows over 26 miles (42 km) from Schengen to Wasserbillig, constitutes the natural border between Luxembourg and Germany. It's divided into two parts. The district of Remich, with its heavy and abundant soil, yields a smooth and harmonious wine. In contrast, the district of Grevenmacher is a region with chalky rocks and slow erosion, producing a pure and elegant wine. The "Cremant de Luxembourg" label was introduced in 1988 exclusively for sparkling wines, which are produced by the "method of Champagne." According to this method, after the grapes are pressed, the juice is allowed to ferment in huge metal vats.

The wine is stirred, sugar and yeast are mixed in, and then it is bottled and corked. The extra sugar and yeast cause a second fermentation in the bottle, which makes the wine fizzy. Sediment is removed and then the bottle is recorked. This method is time-consuming and expensive, but results in a very popular export product.

The wine cellars, six in the Moselle Valley, are open to visitors in the summer months and are popular spots to visit and do some wine tasting. Some of the smaller cellars have become regular meeting spots for the local older folk on Sunday mornings. In the summer it is also possible to travel the "wine river" on board a cruise ship that plies the Moselle River, calling in at the major towns along the way.

SEASONAL FOODS

From March through the end of September, river fish such as trout, pike, and other highly prized small fish from the Sûre, Moselle, and Our Rivers can be found in abundance. Pike is a freshwater game fish that is reputed to kill and eat its own kind. It can grow to as much as 70 pounds (31.8 kg). Those that are usually caught and eaten tend to weigh from 3 to 6 pounds (1.4 to 2.7 kg). The flesh is firm and white, but tends to be dry and coarse, with many sharp bones. Though pike can be cooked in a variety of ways, it is most often used to make stuffing for Quenelles.

Trout is from the same family as salmon. It has a firm, oily flesh and a sweet, delicate flavor. Trout is a good source of protein and contains small amounts of almost every vitamin. The river trout found in Luxembourg has a skin varying in color from silvery-white to dark gray, and is speckled with red, brown, or black spots. The flesh is white in color. The trout is small, so one fish makes a portion for one person. Trout can be cooked either very simply by grilling, frying, or poaching, or used in *Quenelles*.

EATING OUT

Luxembourg City has a great variety of restaurants, representing all tastes, nationalities, and prices. Restaurant food is popular, as it offers an opportunity for dining out, meeting people, and enjoying food that is too difficult or time-consuming to prepare at home. French fries are common, and a selection of vegetables is served with the dishes as integral parts of the meal.

Diners place their order at a busy outdoor restaurant at Place d'Armes in Luxembourg City.

One can choose from Italian or Spanish to Indian, Chinese, or Japanese foods. Pizzerias and Italian cafés are very popular with young people and are often crowded. Also trendy are Spanish restaurants serving tapas (TAH-pahs), snack foods that accompany drinks. Indian restaurants, too, are in vogue.

INTERNET LINKS

http://www.expatica.com/lu/about/Top-foods-in-Luxembourg-with-recipes_507809.html
This site offers a "Top 10" list of traditional Luxembourg foods with photos and links to recipes.

https://www.tripadvisor.com/Restaurants-g190356-Luxembourg_City.html
The wide range of restaurant fare available in Luxembourg City can be seen on this travel site.

BOUNESCHLUPP (GREEN BEAN SOUP)

This comforting soup is said to be a "national dish" of Luxembourg. As such, there are many variations on this recipe, with some adding chopped turnip, celeriac, and/or leeks.

6 slabs thick sliced bacon, diced

1 medium-sized carrot, finely diced

1 small onion, diced

2 cloves garlic, minced

Salt and pepper to taste

4 cups or 1 pound (450 g) fresh green beans, trimmed and cut into bite-sized pieces

2 cups (300 g) waxy potatoes, cut into ½-inch (15 mm) cubes

8 cups (2 liters) beef or chicken broth, stock, or water, or a mixture

1 cup (240 mL) sour cream or crème fraîche

Chives, minced

½ lb (225 g) fully cooked German-style sausage, such as bratwurst or knockwurst (full links)

In a heavy-bottomed Dutch oven, cook bacon over medium heat until browned and crispy. Remove to plate. Add carrots and onion to bacon fat and cook gently until translucent. Add salt and pepper, and stir. Add garlic, beans, potatoes, and most of the bacon (save some for garnish). Cover with broth or water. Bring to a boil, then lower heat to a simmer. Cover pot. Simmer for about 45 minutes or until all vegetables are very tender.

Turn off heat. Bury the sausage in the soup to warm for about 10 minutes. Remove sausage from pot and slice.

Gently stir sour cream into soup. Ladle soup into bowls, top with sliced sausage, reserved bacon, and sprinkle with chives. Serve with crusty bread.

QUETSCHENTAART (LUXEMBOURGISH PLUM TART)

This tart is a treat in the autumn, when prune plums are available. Many Quetschentaarts are made with a yeast crust, but not all. This recipe is a little easier.

½ cup (125 grams) butter, softened
¼ cup (50 grams) sugar
1 egg
1 cup (250g) flour
1 pinch salt
1 ¼ pound (500 grams) fresh damson or Italian prune plums, pitted and cut into six wedges
2 Tbsp powdered sugar

To prepare the dough, beat the butter and sugar in a medium bowl. Add the egg and beat until fluffy. Mix in the flour and salt and form into a firm disk. Wrap in plastic wrap and chill in the refrigerator for 30 minutes.

Meanwhile, preheat the fan oven to 400 degrees Fahrenheit (200° Celsius). Roll out the dough and place it into a buttered, medium-sized pie or tart pan.

Arrange the plum slices in circles on the crust. Bake for 40 minutes or until the fruit is juicy and tender. Let the tart cool. Before serving, sprinkle with powdered sugar. Serve with crème fraîche or whipped cream.

ECONOMIC LUXEMBOURG

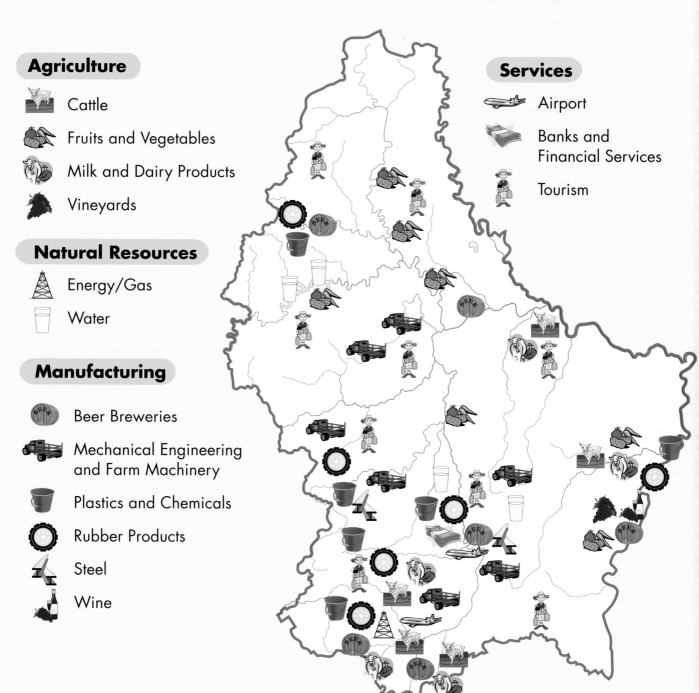

Agriculture

- Cattle
- Fruits and Vegetables
- Milk and Dairy Products
- Vineyards

Natural Resources

- Energy/Gas
- Water

Manufacturing

- Beer Breweries
- Mechanical Engineering and Farm Machinery
- Plastics and Chemicals
- Rubber Products
- Steel
- Wine

Services

- Airport
- Banks and Financial Services
- Tourism

ABOUT THE ECONOMY

LAND AREA
998 square miles (2,585 square km)

LAND USE
Agricultural, 50.7 percent
Forest, 33.5 percent is forest
Other, 15.8 percent

GROSS DOMESTIC PRODUCT (GDP) (official exchange rate)
$60.98 billion (2015)

GDP GROWTH RATE
3.5 percent (2016)

INFLATION RATE
—0.1 percent (2016)

CURRENCY
Euro (€)
Notes: €5, €10, €20, €50, €100, €200, €500
Coins (euro cents): 1c, 2c, 5c, 10c, 20c, 50c, €1, €2
USD 1 = 0.92 euro (March 2017)

GDP BY SECTOR
Agriculture, 0.2 percent; industry, 11 percent; services, 88.7 percent (2016)

GDP PER CAPITA
$102,000 (2016)

WORKFORCE
272,000 (2016)
Note: figure excludes foreign workers; in addition, about 150,000 workers commute daily from France, Belgium, and Germany.

LABOR FORCE BY OCCUPATION
Agriculture, 1.1 percent; industry, 20 percent; services, 78.9 percent (2013)

UNEMPLOYMENT RATE
6.7 percent (2016)

NATURAL RESOURCES
Iron ore (no longer exploited), arable land

AGRICULTURAL PRODUCTS
grapes, barley, oats, potatoes, wheat, fruits; dairy and livestock products

EXPORTS
machinery and equipment, steel products, chemicals, rubber products, glass

MAJOR TRADE PARTNERS
Germany, Belgium, France, China, United States, Netherlands, United Kingdom, Italy, Mexico

CULTURAL LUXEMBOURG

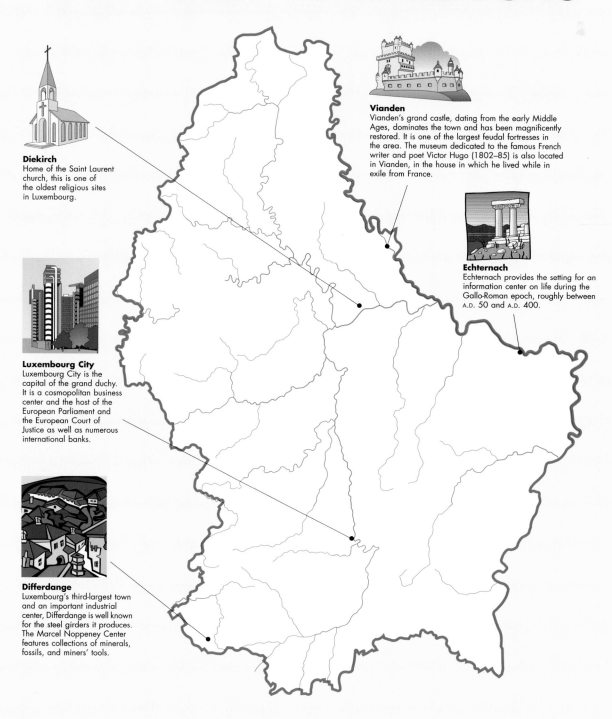

Diekirch
Home of the Saint Laurent church, this is one of the oldest religious sites in Luxembourg.

Vianden
Vianden's grand castle, dating from the early Middle Ages, dominates the town and has been magnificently restored. It is one of the largest feudal fortresses in the area. The museum dedicated to the famous French writer and poet Victor Hugo (1802–85) is also located in Vianden, in the house in which he lived while in exile from France.

Echternach
Echternach provides the setting for an information center on life during the Gallo-Roman epoch, roughly between A.D. 50 and A.D. 400.

Luxembourg City
Luxembourg City is the capital of the grand duchy. It is a cosmopolitan business center and the host of the European Parliament and the European Court of Justice as well as numerous international banks.

Differdange
Luxembourg's third-largest town and an important industrial center, Differdange is well known for the steel girders it produces. The Marcel Noppeney Center features collections of minerals, fossils, and miners' tools.

ABOUT THE CULTURE

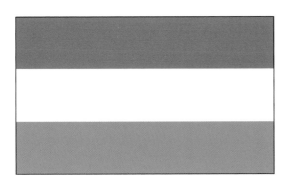

OFFICIAL NAME
Grand Duchy of Luxembourg

POLITICAL STATUS
Constitutional monarchy under a system of parliamentary democracy

FLAG
Rectangular panel with three horizontal stripes of red, white, and blue (from top to bottom)

CAPITAL
Luxembourg City

POPULATION
582,300 (2016)

POPULATION GROWTH RATE
2.05 percent (2016)

BIRTH RATE
11.4 births per 1,000 Luxembourgers (2016)

LIFE EXPECTANCY AT BIRTH
Total, 82.3 years; male, 79.8 years; female, 84.9 years (2016)

INFANT MORTALITY RATE
3.4 deaths /1,000 live births

ETHNIC GROUPS
Luxembourger, 54.1 percent; Portuguese, 16.4 percent; French, 7 percent; Italian, 3.5 percent; Belgian, 3.3 percent; German, 2.3 percent; British, 1.1 percent; other, 12.3 percent

RELIGIONS
Roman Catholicism, 87 percent; Others (Protestantism, Orthodox Christianity, Judaism, and Islam), 13 percent (2000)

LANGUAGES
Luxembourgish, official administrative and judicial language and national language (spoken vernacular), 88.8 percent; French, official administrative, judicial, and legislative language, 4.2 percent; Portuguese, 2.3 percent; German, official administrative and judicial language, 1.1 percent; other 3.5 percent (2011)

TIMELINE

IN LUXEMBOURG	IN THE WORLD
	753 BCE Rome is founded.
	116–17 CE The Roman Empire reaches its greatest extent.
600–700 CE St. Willibrord, an Irish missionary, introduces Christianity in the region.	**600** Height of the Mayan civilization
963 Siegfried begins building castle that will become foundation of Luxembourg.	
1346 Charles of Luxembourg is crowned King of Bohemia and Count of Luxembourg.	
1354 Luxembourg becomes a duchy under Charles IV.	
1400s–1700s Luxembourg and the other Low Countries fall under a succession of foreign rulers—Spain, France, and Austria.	**1776** US Declaration of Independence
	1789–1799 The French Revolution
1815 Luxembourg becomes a Grand Duchy under William I of the Netherlands.	**1869** The Suez Canal is opened.
1890 Grand Duchy of Luxembourg separates from the Netherlands.	
1914–1918 Luxembourg is under German occupation.	**1914–1918** World War I
1940–1944 Luxembourg is occupied by Nazi Germany.	**1939–1945** World War II
1944–1945 Battle of the Bulge.	
1948 Belgium, Luxembourg, and the Netherlands form economic union, Benelux.	**1949** The North Atlantic Treaty Organization (NATO) is formed.

IN LUXEMBOURG	IN THE WORLD
1957 Treaty of Rome; Luxembourg is a founding member of the European Economic Community.	
1964 Duchess Charlotte abdicates in favor of her eldest son, Grand Duke Jean.	**1966–1969** The Chinese Cultural Revolution
	1986 Nuclear power disaster at Chernobyl in Ukraine
1999 The euro is adopted as the official currency in European Union, including Luxembourg.	**1991** Breakup of the Soviet Union
2000 Crown Prince Henri becomes grand duke of Luxembourg on the abdication of his father, Jean.	**2001** Terrorists crash planes in New York, Washington, DC, and Pennsylvania.
2003 University of Luxembourg founded.	**2003** War in Iraq begins.
2004 Prime Minister Jean-Claude Junker's party wins the general election.	
2008 Grand Duke Henri's refusal to sign a bill legalizing euthanasia sparks a constitutional crisis.	**2008** US elects first African American president, Barack Obama.
2009 Luxembourg added to "gray list" of countries with questionable banking practices.	
2013 Xavier Bettel becomes prime minister.	
2014 Luxembourg's parliament votes to legalize same-sex marriage. LuxLeaks scandal breaks.	**2015–2016** ISIS launches terror attacks in Belgium and France.
2017 Black Fountain Press opens Luxembourg's first publishing house for literature written in English.	**2017** Donald Trump becomes US president. Britain begins Brexit process of leaving the EU.

GLOSSARY

Bouneschlupp (BOHN-nen-shlup)
Bean soup

Bretzelsonndeg (BRET-zel-son-deg)
Pretzel Sunday

Burgbrennen (BURG-bren-en)
Bonfire Day, an end-of-winter custom performed in February

Émaischen (Eh-MAY-schen)
Traditional market held on Easter Monday in Luxembourg City

Fierkelsjhelli (fear-KUL-hel-la)
Roasted suckling pig covered in an aspic.

Hammelsmarsch (HAMM-els-marsh)
The sheep's march, a lively tune played during the shepherds' market.

Housecker (HUSE-eck-er)
Father Christmas's companion

Jaudes (YOW-des)
A dog rose bush covered in paper flowers and multicolored ribbons, made for the Rattles Round

Judd mat Gaardebounen (Yudd mat gard-DUH-born-nen)
Smoked neck of pork in herb sauce, with broad beans and boiled potatoes

Kachkéis (KARCH-kays)
Soft and sticky boiled cheese

Kiermes (KEER-mes)
Village fair held on the anniversary of the local saint

Kleeschen (CLE-schen)
Father Christmas

Klibberegoen (KLI-bare-gurn)
Rattles Round, where children go through the streets, using rattles to remind people of Mass in the three days leading up to Easter Sunday

Kuddelfleck (KU-del-fleck)
Boiled tripe

Liichteméss (LICH-ter-mess)
End-of-winter ritual celebrated in February

Miertchen (MI-air-shen)
Saint Martin's Fire, an ancient end of harvest celebration

Quenelles (keh-nells)
Small oval-shaped meat or fish dumplings

Schueberfouer (SHOO-bare-foor)
Former shepherds' market, now a giant amusement park in the capital

Stiefesdag (SHTEEF-fes-dag)
Saint Stephen's Day, the day after Christmas, also called Boxing Day

FOR FURTHER INFORMATION

BOOKS

DK Eyewitness Travel Guide: Belgium & Luxembourg. New York: DK Publishing, 2015.

Eccardt, Thomas M. *Secrets of the Seven Smallest States of Europe*. New York: Hippocrene Books, 2005.

Skelton, Tim. *Luxembourg, Bradt Travel Guide*. Guilford, Conn.: Globe Pequot Press, 2015.

ONLINE

BBC News. Luxembourg country profile. http://www.bbc.com/news/world-europe-17548470

CIA World Factbook. Luxembourg. https://www.cia.gov/library/publications/the-world-factbook/geos/lu.html

European Union. https://europa.eu/european-union/index_en

Luxembourg, Official Portal of the Grand Duchy of. http://www.luxembourg.public.lu/en

Luxembourger Wort. http://www.wort.lu/en

US Department of State on Luxembourg. www.state.gov/r/pa/ei/bgn/3182.h

BIBLIOGRAPHY

CIA World Factbook, Luxembourg. https://www.cia.gov/library/publications/the-world-factbook/geos/lu.html

Fox, Joel. "This Luxembourg town treated me like a VIP because of my father's WWII heroics to liberate it from Nazis." *The Washington Post,* September 22, 2014. https://www.washingtonpost.com/posteverything/wp/2014/09/22/this-luxembourg-town-treated-me-like-a-vip-because-of-my-fathers-wwii-heroics-to-liberate-it-from-nazis/?utm_term=.db7f9ee3f87b

Guarascio, Francesco. "EU offers new plan to tackle corporate tax dodging." Reuters, April 12, 2016. http://www.reuters.com/article/us-panama-tax-eu-idUSKCN0X91G9

Israely, Jeff. "Luxembourg's Monarch Steps Back on Euthanasia Bill." *Time*, December 12, 2008. http://content.time.com/time/world/article/0,8599,1865825,00.html

Luxembourger Wort. "Women in Luxembourg earn more than men, study finds." January 14, 2013. http://www.wort.lu/en/luxembourg/women-in-luxembourg-earn-more-than-men-study-finds-50f435dfe4b0092f07fcc80a

Luxembourger Wort. "The most popular baby names in Luxembourg of 2015." December 29, 2015. http://www.wort.lu/en/luxembourg/what-s-in-a-name-the-most-popular-baby-names-in-luxembourg-of-2015-56829a190da165c55dc504e8?utm_campaign=magnet&utm_source=article_page&utm_medium=related_articles

Luxembourger Wort. "Introducing Luxembourg's new 'Lentille' stadium." November 24, 2016. http://www.wort.lu/en/sport/60-million-euros-introducing-luxembourg-s-new-lentille-stadium-5836eb745061e01abe83ca7e

Luxembourger Wort. "Luxembourg City population exceeds 110,000." February 24, 2016. http://www.wort.lu/en/luxembourg/population-luxembourg-city-population-exceeds-110-000-56cd7e151bea9dff8fa7368f#

Shaxson, Nicholas. "Explainer: what is a tax haven?" *The Guardian*, January 9, 2011. https://www.theguardian.com/business/2011/jan/09/explainer-what-is-tax-haven

INDEX

INDEX

© Aladdin Books Ltd 1999
Produced by
Aladdin Books Ltd
28 Percy Street
London W1P 0LD

First published in the United States in 1999 by
Copper Beech Books,
an imprint of
The Millbrook Press
2 Old New Milford Road
Brookfield, Connecticut 06804

Concept, editorial, and design by
David West Children's Books

Designer: Flick Killerby

Editor: Liz White

Library of Congress Cataloging-in-Publication Data
The encyclopedia of our awesome earth.
p. cm.
Includes index.
Summary: Provides information about geological and weather
phenomena such as tornadoes, earthquakes, volcanoes, tidal waves,
thunder clouds, blizzards, and weather prediction.
ISBN 0-7613-0831-8
1. Earth sciences Miscellanea Juvenile literature.
[1. Earth sciences Miscellanea.]
QE29.E53 1999   99-39169
550–dc21   CIP
Printed in Belgium

5 4 3

THE

ENCYCLOPEDIA

—— OF OUR ——

awesome

EARTH